THE ROMAN REPUBLIC

By

Henry C. Boren

New York - D. Van Nostrand Co.

Copyright date 1965

THE WONDERSMITHS

BY

Henry C. Jordan

New York - D. Van Nostrand Co.

Copyright 1936

PREFACE

In the early chapters of this volume the author has steered rather carefully through the Scylla and Charybdis of controversy, in the belief that the literary tradition cannot be wholly discounted (and in any case was a factor in Roman history) and that the archaeological remains must be interpreted within the general framework of the tradition. There is no commitment, however, to the view that the middle ground is always right.

In the middle chapters (especially 6, 7, and 8) it is hoped that even the professional historian will find fresh treatment and emphases which may give new and meaningful insight. Social and economic information has been used to the full.

It would be impossible to give credit to all whose work has influenced the writer. Tenney Frank is one who above all should be singled out as having stimulated thought and contributed to understanding. Inevitably one accepts many of the views of his teachers. Thus Professor Joseph Ward Swain of the University of Illinois, in his informed, thought-provoking lectures, has exercised no little influence in an indirect way upon this volume. The editor of this series, Professor Louis L. Snyder of the City College of New York, gave the manuscript a most careful reading and helped to eliminate undesirable stylistic variations. The writer, certainly, cannot pass on to others any responsibility for errors of interpretation or of fact.

H.C.B.

TABLE OF CONTENTS

Part I—THE ROMAN REPUBLIC

3

Part II—READINGS

Part I

THE ROMAN REPUBLIC

— 1 —

INTRODUCTION

Why Study Roman History? One reason why the history of Rome has been fascinating to generations of historians is that it is a relatively complete unit. In fairly well documented form it is possible to see how a tiny city-state rose to world power and then declined. The visual traces of Rome's greatness are still seen in magnificent ruins which are scattered from the Near East to Western Europe and Britain. How could a world empire which produced such impressive buildings, bridges and aqueducts, so successful that it endured century after century, nonetheless come to an end so final? Scholars who have worked out cyclical theories of history have usually begun with Rome. Her experience became, for them, the model system by which other empires and civilizations are judged.

But the lessons of Rome are not universal. History can never repeat itself: the factors in given historical contexts are never exactly the same. Yet generalizations and parallels, if carefully used, may illuminate the present, and Rome furnishes her share of these. For twentieth-century America it may well be argued that the most profitable of these parallels are found in the Republic rather than the Empire. Are not the growth and decline of semipopular institutions such as assemblies and jury-courts more significant for us than the tribulations of a

7

centralized absolutism? Again, however, the student must not expect the Roman experience to be directly applicable in the modern world. In fact, one of the most valuable lessons he may learn from history is that he should discount heavily the dire predictions made by politicians (usually those out of power) when the past is called up as a witness to imminent disaster. The study of history may impart a kind of general wisdom useful in judging contemporary affairs; for in some ways man has not changed much in spite of the tremendous outward alterations accomplished through science and industry.

The history of Rome is worth studying as a thing in itself. Here were stable institutions, great men, worthy achievement. Here also, to be sure, were crudeness and brutality, militarism and imperialism, and failure as well as success. Roman ways do not seem strange. We can get to know the Romans—so well that scholars tend to become bound up with great figures such as Cicero or Caesar, and to quarrel indignantly over their merits or lack of them. This familiarity may be less real than we think. Even enlightened men like Cicero were profoundly influenced by a tradition—including some rather primitive ideas, as in religion—which we can never completely capture nor completely understand. But this is the fate of all historical research; in the nature of things it must be incomplete and imperfect.

The Raw Materials of Roman History. The historian today finds it most difficult to discern the objective facts of Roman history. It is especially troublesome to deal with the legends of early Rome. There exist almost no written records dated earlier than the second century B.C. The best of the ancient historians, notably Livy and Dionysius Halicarnassus, wrote in the first century B.C. Their sources of information were seldom more than a century and a half old. Some ancient materials were available to them, such as lists of magistrates, inscriptions with texts of treaties, and a law code, but they did not always make use of them. Further, when the city was burned about 387 B.C. such records may have been destroyed and afterward faultily reconstructed.

The modern historian usually cannot double-check the work of the Roman historians of antiquity. He must to an extraordinary degree rely upon his own judgment and upon scraps of information for the account he presents. The student must bear in mind that what he reads about the Romans is third-hand or worse. The facts have been filtered through selection and sometimes through rhetorical treatment both by the ancient and by the modern authors. The ancient writers in a general way were attempting to explain to their own people Rome's greatness in terms of men and developing institutions. These writers believed that Rome rose to dominance because of certain traits of character and certain wise policies—fidelity to family and state, tolerance, discipline, perseverance, thriftiness, humanitarianism—and a corresponding lack of their opposites. They emphasized the stories and personalities which exemplified these virtues. It might be added that almost invariably they believed their own age to be deficient in these virtues.

The historian today may—perhaps must—accept to some extent these judgments of their colleagues of a couple of millennia past. However, he will also search and sift all the evidence in order to give emphasis to other forces which men consider important today. These new emphases include economic development, social change, and intellectual growth. Unfortunately, these sections of his work will be less factual and more a matter of interpretive reconstruction than writer or reader could wish. The conscientious historian, then, fully aware of his own limitations and those of his evidence, tries to establish what is important to men of the twentieth century; but he also attempts to recapture the essential spirit of the age.

EARLY ITALY

Topography and Climate. Rome's history was influenced, of course, by geography. Italy, welded to the continent at the Alps, juts southeast 650 miles into the Mediterranean. The spine of the peninsula, the Apennine range, attaches to the Alps in the northwest at Liguria, leaving room for the great river valley of the Po. The Adriatic sea separates Italy from Illyria (approximately modern Yugoslavia and Albania) on the east. To the west lies the Tyrrhenian sea. The Apennines, with some peaks which rise about 9,000 feet, divide east from west rather sharply. In central Italy the mountains range toward the east; the western coast is better favored: the rivers are longer, the farmland better. In the center, on the Tiber, the largest river south of the Po, lies Rome. The area is known as Latium, for here dwelled the Latin peoples, thirty by tradition. Rome was founded on a strategic spot far enough up the Tiber to be relatively safe from pirate attacks. The river was navigable up to the city for boats of medium size, which were towed from the banks.

The climate is generally pleasant. Winters are wet and chilly, summers dry and hot. Romans of means always tried to get out of the city to the surrounding hill country in midsummer. Southern Italy is more often subjected to the dry, hot African winds, while in the north, winds off the Alps may be freezing cold. Sudden storms are a characteristic of the region, and even in the earliest historical period Latin farmers diligently provided underground drainage to prevent erosion.

In modern times Italy seems not to have the resources —coal, oil, iron, uranium—and population which are necessary to first-rank world power. To the ancients, however, Italy was a well-endowed and rich area. (*See Reading No. 1.*) Latium and Etruria (Tuscany), northwest along the coast, are both relatively productive and in antiquity furnished some iron, copper, tin, and zinc. To the south lay Campania, the richest farmland south of the Po. In these areas, which together comprise west-central Italy, the highest cultures penetrated and the strongest political units were established. Southeast from Rome lay rugged Samnium, then Apulia and Calabria at the tip of the peninsula. West from there around the gulf of Tarentum are Lucania and Bruttium, which is separated from Sicily only by the narrow Strait of Messina. North of Rome along the Ariatic lay Umbria.

Italy Before Rome. Italy and the western Mediterranean lagged far behind the ancient East. In the third millennium B.C., when great bronze age civilizations were flowering in Mesopotamia, in Egypt, and in the Indus river valley, Italy could boast only modest neolithic villages. The iron age also came to the East several centuries before it did to Rome. By the sixth century B.C. pre-eminence in cultural achievement had passed to Greece. By the beginning of the Christian era Rome's own achievements were outstanding enough to make it proper to speak of "Greco-Roman" civilization.

Little needs to be said here about neolithic Italy. Literally hundreds of neolithic village sites are known, many of them from aerial photographs taken during and after World War II. Variation in the growth of vegetation at these sites shows quite clearly in these photographs. The round, wattle-and-daub houses were dug into the ground a foot or two. In the center of the house was a hearth; directly above it was a hole for ventilation. The photographs show the houses grouped together, perhaps originally for protection. They were surrounded by a ditch or ditches. Where excavated, these sites yield typical tools and potsherds.

During the bronze age (after about 1800 B.C.) new immigrants into north Italy developed a more advanced culture known as Terremare (from a dialectical modern term for their refuse heaps). They built post-frame houses both round and oblong, and sometimes perched on piles like those of the lake-dwellers farther to the north. A few sites indicate town planning on a rectangular or square grid pattern. To the south in the same period was developing another bronze age culture called the Apennine. The Apennine people buried their dead (Terre-marans cremated theirs) and produced a black, geo-metrically decorated pottery. Apennine remains have been found at the lowest levels in Rome, but for some reason bronze age cultures did not flourish in west-central Italy.

The best known culture in Italy in the early iron age (after 900 B.C.) is called Villanovan, after a principal site in North Italy near Bologna. Since the Villanovans also cremated (later they sometimes inhumed), some scholars have argued that they descended from the Terre-mare people. Others have postulated a new invasion. A great variety of vases, ornaments of precious metals, and other artifacts are dug from Villanovan sites, which extend from the Po to the lower Tiber on the western side of the peninsula. Sometimes the Villanovans buried the ashes of their dead in little "hut-urns" which model for us the round or oval huts in which they lived. In the archaeological strata on Tuscan sites the southern Villa-novan culture immediately precedes the Etruscan.

The Etruscans. In some ways the Etruscans are a mysterious people, both attractive and frustrating to scholars. Their culture appears in Etruria by 700 B.C., already full and rich and apparently without antecedent. Their origins were argued by scholars in antiquity as in modern times. The most widely held view is that they migrated from Asia Minor and moved into Tuscany during the eighth century B.C. (*See Reading No. 2.*) Re-ligious practices such as taking the omens by studying livers of animals, certain features of their art, and ancient evidence seem to corroborate this theory of their origin, but there are dissident factors also. Those scholars who believe that the Etruscans were indigenous or that they came from the north or from the east across the Adriatic may one day be proved right.

If the Etruscan language could be understood and classified, the relationships would perhaps give a defini-tive clue. Since the Etruscans mostly used the Greek alphabet, the writing itself presents no problem. Many of the meanings of words are known through ancient evidence and through inference. Even the basic prin-ciples of grammar have been ingeniously worked out. But still the full grasp of the language eludes the scholars. And final success may bring disappointment, for there is no extant literature and most inscriptions are short, usually epitaphs.

The Etruscans were able to dominate most of central and northern Italy by the sixth century B.C. They were great traders, and theirs was a maritime as well as land power. Their marvelous underground tomb chambers reveal the degree of their prosperity and security, especially in the sixth century B.C. The finest Greek pottery and other objects of art were brought in, and they had the money and the leisure to develop a great art of their own. Apparently, the income to pay for these imports derived from agriculture and smelting of metals. The Etruscans were never numerous enough to occupy all the territories they dominated; they merely installed themselves as the ruling aristocracy.

Etruscan power was not highly centralized. A federalized league of twelve cities controlled Tuscany, and similar leagues, perhaps also of groups of twelve cities, were established in the Po valley and in central Italy south of Tuscany. While one city might prosper and become more populous than the rest, its priest-king (*lucumon*) never became powerful enough to gain control of the entire federation. The federation itself was loosely organized. Federal activities were directed by a council in which the twelve cities were equally represented. The supreme head of the league (*rex*) apparently had little power. Action was therefore limited to those projects upon which the council could agree. In the period of Etruscan decline after about 500 B.C., city-states like Rome profited from Etruscan disunity.

The binding spirit of the federation was religious more than political. Headquarters in Etruria were at the shrine of the god Voltumna at a site which the Romans called Volsinii. The annual ceremonies and games held here were the high occasion of the Etruscan year. The political conferences of the *lucumones* at the time of the festival seem to have been secondary. Religion also played an important role within each city-state. The *lucumon* was priest as well as king; he acted only with the guidance of the gods shown through omens read by the *haruspices*. Probably the ruler was himself the chief *haruspex*. Besides the examination of livers (hepatoscopy) and the entrails of animals, the omens were taken through observation of the skies (augury). A kind of grid was laid out, and the flights of birds and other phenomena were noted in relation to it.

These practices of reading the omens were adopted by the early Romans. Romans also built Etruscan-like temples with three *cellae*; one such was the temple to Jupiter, Juno, and Minerva, Roman names for chief Etruscan deities. From them they learned surveying and town-planning. Gladiatorial combat was apparently an Etruscan import. Some officials and even institutions like the Roman Senate may have been Etruscan in origin. The Romans themselves acknowledged their debt to the Etruscans, and Roman scholars studied Etruscan lore. The Emperor Claudius wrote works on their history and language, all unfortunately lost. It is possible to over-emphasize Etruscan influence. The Etruscans were themselves much influenced, especially in art, by the Greeks.

The Greeks in Italy. The second culturally advanced people the Romans encountered as they struggled toward dominance in the western Mediterranean was the Greeks. They entered Italy a little later than the Etruscans. According to tradition, the first Greek colony in Italy was at Cumae, founded about 750 B.C. The Greeks occupied so much of south Italy that the Romans called this area *Magna Graecia*. Principal cities included Thurii, Tarentum, Paestum, and Croton. The Greeks also occupied much of the eastern half of Sicily (where Syracuse became the chief city), a portion of Sardinia, and areas in southern France and eastern Spain. In cultural, intellectual, and political achievement these city-states were not far behind the leading cities of the Greek homeland. Names like Pythagoras and Archimedes are associated with the Greek west.

The Carthaginians. A third state powerful in the western Mediterranean was Carthage. Its influence on Rome was perhaps less than that of either the Greeks or the Etruscans, and later, but in the area of agriculture, for example, it was important. Carthage was a Phoenician colony supposedly established about 800 B.C. Archaeologists have found nothing earlier than about 725 B.C. With the decline of the Phoenician cities Carthage became dominant in all the areas of Phoenician penetration: they controlled much of north Africa, western Sicily, and southern Spain. Carthaginians and Etruscans often fought against the Greeks, sometimes in alliance. Rome was destined to vanquish them all.

The Founding of Rome. The stories told by the Romans about the founding of the city and its early history are a motley combination of legend and fact. The ancient Roman historians repeated the stories with a general credulity; they did attempt to reconcile conflicting elements, rationalize some supernatural points, and warn of possible fabrications. The fullest extant accounts are to be found in Livy and Dionysius Halicarnassus. Modern historians, of course, question the traditional stories, and, indeed, in the skeptical and confident nineteenth century, historians tended to reject them as entirely fabulous. Since then, scholars have learned that such legendary tales generally have a basis in fact. Today's historians try to discern the factual fabric behind the accumulated embroidery.

The tradition links the founding of Rome with the more ancient civilizations of the east. The ancestor of Romulus was Aeneas, who fled burning Troy. Guided by fate or the gods and in spite of his own desires (his mission broke up a torrid love affair with Dido) Aeneas was brought inexorably to Latium. He married into the family of the local chieftain. Fate still worked in his descendants toward the destined establishment. Not even the scheming of a rascally uncle could extinguish the lives of the twin sons of Rhea Silvia (a Vestal virgin) and the god Mars. They were exposed to die in a basket on the Tiber, but were nursed by a wolf and then reared by a shepherd. On reaching maturity they learned of their origin and slew the uncle. It was Romulus who founded the first settlement at Rome on the Palatine and who gave the city its name. Romulus fortified his site and "eternal Rome" was founded. The year was 753 B.C. (*See Reading No. 3A.*)

Modern archaeology confirms the tradition in an approximate way. The Palatine does seem to have been occupied first. Although there are some earlier human remains, it appears that the middle eighth century as a date for the establishment of a real village (distinctly not a city) is about right. However, the traditional events are of interest primarily because they show us what Romans of the last centuries of the Republic thought about their own past.

— 3 —

ROME UNDER THE MONARCHY

Early Kings: The Traditional Tales. In the accounts of Rome's seven kings left to us (mostly from the late Republic) the monarchs tend to be stereotyped as conquerors, lawgivers, or organizers. The first king, Romulus, was a conqueror. He expanded the Roman dominions and population. He was also reported to have made his new city a refuge for exiles and questionable characters. Because the Sabines wanted no Romans for sons-in-law, these early Romans arranged the "rape of the Sabines."

Numa Pompilius, the second king, was actually a Sabine. He was typed as a peaceful organizer, the founder of state religious orders and ceremonies, something of a lawgiver. Tullus Hostilius, third of the monarchs, was even more militaristic than Romulus himself. He was said to have extended Rome's dominions in Latium, destroyed the mother city, Alba Longa, and annexed its territory and people. Ancus Marcius gave careful attention to the religious observances, as might have been expected from a grandson of Numa. He also (it is said) built the Pons Sublicius (Pile Bridge) over the Tiber. Moreover, probably for the sake of the salt-works, he established a colony at Ostia, which would one day become Rome's major port.

Etruscan Kings of Rome. The last three kings of Rome were apparently Etruscan. The evidence for a period of Etruscan domination is strong, even though the first two of the "Etruscan" kings are said to have waged war against Etruscan towns. Lucius Tarquinius Priscus, according to the Roman historians, came from Etruria (though they thought that he was Greek). Livy called him "Lucumo," an Etruscan title. At his accession he appears as something of a champion of the lower classes. He promoted commoners to the ranks both of the

16

nobility and of the class which furnished the cavalry. His construction in Rome included a temple to Jupiter and perhaps the *cloaca maxima,* a sewer which drained the forum area. He led successful military campaigns against the Sabines and a whole series of Latin towns.

Servius Tullius, sixth of Rome's kings, was, it was said, brought up in the house of Tarquin. On the assassination of Tarquin, Tullius, aided by Tanaquil, wife of Tarquin, became king. The sons of Tarquin were thus passed over. (Probably they were really grandsons and were too young to rule.) Servius was remembered as the organizer of the class structure. In a manner quite usual in antiquity he classified the Romans in relation to their position in the army, that is, on the basis of property, the amount of military equipment each could afford. This action was somewhat analogous to the work of the Athenian Solon, carried out only a few years earlier, if the traditional dates are accurate. The "leading" citizens—that is, those both rich and well-born—supplied the cavalry. The infantry in the first class was heavily armed and armored. Four more classes of troops ranged downward to the slingers and buglers. Men so poor that they ranked below the fifth infantry class were exempt from military service. Servius was also credited with turning this army organization into a political assembly, but this probably came later. (*See p. 24.*) Servius was said to have walled the city, probably with earthwork (*agger*) faced with stone.

The last of the kings was Lucius Tarquinius Superbus (the "Proud"), descended from Priscus and married to Tullia, daughter of Servius. The Romans had little that was good to say about him from his accession, when he killed the king his father-in-law, until he was dethroned. Tullia was also evil: she ran a chariot over her father's dead body. Tarquin was said to have put to death without trial even senators. He ruled by fear. He was successful in foreign conquests, but shifty and cunning there also.

The incident which supposedly led to his exile was his son's rape of the fair matron Lucretia, wife of another Tarquin. The lady proved her own innocence by committing suicide after the harrowing tale was told. The George Washington of the Romans, Lucius Junius Brutus, avenged Lucretia and drove out the Tarquins, including the late lady's own husband. Chosen magistrate of the new Republic, Brutus successfully organized the defense against the inevitable counterattack. The monarchy was ended. Traditionally, the date was 509 B.C.

Modern Views of the Traditional Monarchy. The foregoing paragraphs indicate that little credence can be given to the details of the tradition. That there was a monarchy we need not doubt. An archaeological discovery from the Roman forum, an early inscription found below the *"Lapis niger,"* mentions the word king. The stone marked a tabooed spot or sacred place. It is not impossible that the traditional list is accurate and the dates approximately so.

If there was a Romulus, he ruled over a mud-hut village and not anything that could be called a city, much less a real "state." The *curiate* organization ascribed to him must be Etruscan. Archaeologists have unearthed nothing at Ostia which could date back to Ancus Marcius. Not until the sixth century B.C. did Rome have a satisfactory drain for the swampy forum, pebble-paved streets, or a wall of any consequence. Archaeological evidence of continued Etruscan influence down to around mid-fifth century is taken by some scholars to mean that the Republic was founded a half-century later than the traditional date. However, the *fasti* (magistrate lists) give names of consuls back to the late sixth century and tend to support tradition.

What the Romans thought about their past influenced them just as powerfully as if these stories had been the exact truth. Romans of the late Republic thought that a broad tolerance toward foreigners and a willingness to accept ideas and institutions from them helped Rome rise to greatness. They retained a hatred for kings and the trappings of monarchy. (*See Reading No. 3B.*) Aristocrats were suspicious of any of their own number who courted popularity even through personal charity, like Servius Tullius. Romans felt that even the most powerful men must be subject to the law. Such convictions, taught to Romans from earliest childhood, were given vivid color and substance in these partly factual legends and traditions.

— 4 —

THE EARLY REPUBLIC

Struggle for Survival. The early years of the Republic were difficult ones. Because of her location Rome had prospered under the Etruscans. Now, after the first quarter of the fifth century B.C., she suffered an economic decline from which she did not soon emerge. During this time the Etruscans attempted to regain dominance. There were critical struggles with the Sabines, Aequians, and Volscians. By 400 B.C. the Romans had subdued some of their more belligerent neighbors. About 396 (traditional date) they took the Etruscan fortress city of Veii, across the Tiber and a few miles north of Rome. The Etruscans had been weakened by repeated irruptions of Celts into the Po region perhaps beginning shortly before 400 B.C.

Rome Captured and Burned, 387 B.C. The Gauls (as the Romans called them) from the Po valley made raids into Etruria and down the Tiber. A Roman army met them at the Allia river near the Tiber and was routed. Rome was looted and burned. Only the citadel held out. The Gauls exacted a heavy money payment and retired northward. M. Furius Camillus, legendary military hero and conqueror of Veii, was made dictator in the crisis, and soon the Romans avenged themselves on the Gauls. With Rome in ashes, some citizens favored abandoning the site and rebuilding on the more easily fortified heights of Veii. But Camillus persuaded the Romans to rebuild. The city was not sacked again for eight hundred years.

Roman Society in the Early Republic. Early society in Rome was rural. The patrician aristocrats were large landowners. Each such family or clan (*gens*)—there were only fifty or sixty of them—had numerous clients, free men but somehow dependent on their patrons. We are told that the Claudius who headed the last great family added to the patrician ranks was patron to several thousand clients. The figure is probably exaggerated. The patron had the obligation of protecting his clients' rights, especially in matters of law. Clients, in turn, supported the patron in various ways. The relationship was formal and hereditary. (*See Reading No. 3C.*)

Plebeians included the clients and all other citizens who were not patricians. Most were small farmers who knew how to endure hardship and austerity. Their small acreages they made as self-sufficient as possible. Many of them lived in mud-and-wattle huts still, possessing only the barest necessities. As Rome expanded the plebeian ranks came to encompass also rich and influential persons. By the middle and late Republic the plebeian class was diverse indeed.

Early Roman Religion. A rural society, naturally enough, produced a rural religion. The Bona Dea, an earth-mother, and Ceres, goddess of grain, were early important. The major household gods were Vesta, goddess of the hearth, and the Lares and Penates. These were also state gods, protecting the state hearth and state storehouses. Other prominent state gods—some derived from Etruscan or Greek influences—included Jupiter, Juno, Minerva, and Mars. The earlier Romans conceived of their gods as local spirits (*numina*). Anthropomorphic conceptions they picked up later from Etruscans and Greeks.

In the early Republic there already existed several priestly colleges for the state gods. The members were laymen (for many years patricians), nominated by the chief priest (*pontifex maximus*) or chosen by the present members through coöptation. Most important were the college of pontiffs, the flamens of Jupiter and Mars, the Vestal Virgins, and the augurs. The augurs took the auspices and therefore had some political prestige. Besides exercising a general supervision, the *pontifex maximus* kept certain state records, the *annales maximi*, and was in charge of the calendar. He, therefore, determined on what days business could be transacted (*dies fasti*) and added an intercalary month approximately every other year to make the essentially lunar calendar correspond with the solar year.

Among both patricians and plebeians the family was important. The *pater familias*, ruling not just the immediate family but also married sons, daughters-in-law, and grandchildren, was very powerful and respected. The *patria potestas* even permitted the father to put to death his own children. Though this of course was a rarity there was one instance even in the late Republic.

The Struggle of the Orders. The Roman historians of the later Republic (*see pp. 8f*), upon whom we must in large part still depend, had much to say about the Struggle of the Orders (patricians and plebeians). On one or more occasions large bodies of plebeians are said to have seceded from Rome in order to gain concessions. The patricians had led the rebellion against the Etruscans, and they dominated the early Republican political structure. Reaction against this patrician monopoly of the government was one part of the struggle. Another cause was the economic decline following the withdrawal of Etruscan trade. The ancient writers emphasized agitation over extensive debt, high interest rates, and the sale of debtors into slavery.

A third and important cause was military. The last three kings, needing more men for the army, may have offended the patricians by attempting to give political privileges to some plebeians. The expulsion of the kings did not alter the military need. Plebeians wealthy enough to afford the armor of the heavy infantry were in a position to bargain. The conflict sometimes took the form of a refusal of eligible plebeians to serve in the army. Patricians resorted to invasion scare-stories or to the extraordinary powers of the dictatorship to enforce the draft. Again, the military side to the struggle is seen in the development of the army formations into a political assembly (*see p. 24*) in which citizens ranked according to their importance in the army.

Fully as important as the military factor was the enlargement of the upper ranks of the plebeian order through expansion. Many wealthy and powerful persons, no doubt including some who had been aristocrats in their own towns, became Roman. Since the patriciate (until Julius Caesar) could be entered only by birth, they became merely plebeians. Such men could not long be subordinated. Using the army as a lever, these leaders gradually gained for all of their order a higher political status. Our information is not sure enough to permit a firm chronological account of the Struggle of the Orders. Both ancient and modern historians have used the technique of reasoning backward from the known results of the struggle. To those results we now turn.

Social and Legal Equality. According to tradition one early plebeian gain was the right of appeal (*provocatio*) from the magistrates to the assembly of the people in capital cases. Another achievement was the first codified and written law, the XII Tables. Patricians had previously controlled the legal system and presumably "remembered" the law. In 451 (traditional date) a decemvirate, or board of ten men, was established. For two years they superseded all the upper magistrates while they codified the law. Probably a written law weakened the basis of the patron-client system, although in gradually changing form this system remained important throughout the Republic.

The XII Tables, according to the accounts, were drawn up after a study of Greek codes like that of Solon in Athens. Archaeological evidence showing early Greek influence in Rome makes this seem more likely than used to be thought. The code itself contained some clauses that seem far from enlightened. The XII Tables became the foundation for the later development of Roman civil and criminal law, one of the most important legacies of Rome to the modern world. (*See Reading No. 10.*)

Another legal tussle was ended by the *Lex Canuleia* (traditional date 445 B.C.), which legalized marriage between patricians and plebeians. The aim here was only partly social, for the legal right to will and inherit property was doubtless what was desired.

The Political Side of the Struggle. According to tradition, the first important political demand of the plebeians resulted (492 B.C.) in the establishment of a new officer, the tribune of the plebs. From an early date there were ten of these officials, whose chief function was to safeguard plebeian rights. By 471 (traditionally) a new assembly of the people, the *concilium plebis,* excluding patricians, had been organized to elect the new officials. Plebeian *aediles,* keepers of certain temples, seem to have played some role in the struggle. Later conflicts centered about the authority of this assembly and about the demands of plebeians to be eligible to other magistracies early monopolized by the patricians.

It is puzzling that the existing *fasti consulares* (lists of consuls) contain some plebeian names in the earliest period when according to the literary sources they were not eligible for the consulship. The accounts have it that when plebeian agitation mounted the patricians agreed to set up a new office, military tribune with consular power, to which the plebeians were eligible. And the *fasti* do show that in most of the years between 444 and 367 B.C. the consuls were replaced by these officials (usually several of them). After 367 B.C., the consulship again became the chief magistracy. The sources say that the Licinian-Sextian laws of that year required that one of the consuls must be plebeian. Again, however, the consular lists after this date show that some years both were patrician.

Other plebeian gains include eligibility to the quaestorship (421 B.C.), to the dictatorship (356 B.C.), to the censorship (351 B.C.), to the praetorship (337 B.C.), to the curule aedileship (304 B.C.), and to the priestly colleges (300 B.C.). Traditionally, the Senate held a virtual veto over the *leges* and *plebescita* of the primary assemblies. It may be doubted whether in the earliest period the Senate was actually so powerful. In any case, the accounts emphasize that the centuriate assembly in 339 and the tribunal assembly in 287 (by the Publilian and Hortensian laws) gained the power to pass legislation without approval of the Senate.

It would be a mistake to think that now Rome had become a real democracy. Plebeians elected to the top offices were usually not of the lower economic stratum. More likely than not their interests corresponded with those of the patricians. The latter accepted those plebeians who reached the top into a broadened aristocracy (*nobilitas*). Moreover, there were numerous ways of controlling men and votes. The assemblies could not meet frequently. The Roman government remained a government of magistrates who felt themselves responsible to the Roman people only in a paternal sense. They consulted with their fellow aristocrats in the Senate and usually followed their advice. Rome was, then, an aristocratic oligarchy still. But the oligarchy had been broadened by the struggle of the orders.

The Roman Constitution: A Summary. The chief elective and legislative body of the early Republic was the centuriate assembly (*comitia centuriata*), in which citizens were ranked according to their army classification. (*See p. 17.*) Tradition credited it to Servius Tullius, but it was more likely the work of the fifth century. Citizens were placed into 193 centuries according to wealth (which gave to the oligarchy a timocratic aspect). At the top were the cavalry centuries. Below that came five classes of infantry. There were a few centuries of supernumeraries and one century of propertyless *proletarii*. The numbers of persons in the top centuries were less than in the others. Voting was by century and oral. Within the century the votes of *seniores* (those over 45 years of age) counted as heavily as those of the more numerous *iuniores*. The cavalry centuries always voted first, then the first class of infantry, and so on. When a majority was reached, the voting stopped.

The assembly of tribes (*comitia tributa*) was organized on a somewhat more democratic basis. Each tribe (by the middle Republic there were four city and thirty-one rural tribes) was based on a geographic area. Voting was by tribe, the order determined by lot. Like the centuriate assembly, the tribal assembly included all citizens. However, patricians presumably withdrew when tribunes of the plebs were chosen. Once the tribal assembly gained the independent right to pass legislation (*see p. 23*) it could play a larger, potentially even predominant, role. The social structure, especially the patron-client system, and the fact that most tribunes were upper-level plebeians prevented any such tendency until the late Republic.

The Senate, a body of about 300, was made up generally of ex-magistrates, who were members for life. The constitutional position of the Senate was somewhat ambiguous. Technically, the will of the whole people expressed in assembly superseded any other authority. However, the assemblies were cumbersome and could not be called together quickly. The Senate could meet frequently. It contained a great reservoir of experienced men. Magistrates consulted it and followed its advice. The senatorial authority (*auctoritas patrum*) was thus ordinarily very great. The senatorial decree (*senatus consultum*) usually had the force of law. In the middle Republic, when Roman armies fought on several fronts and important decisions had to be made daily, the actual power of the Senate increased. It supervised the treasury, gave assignments to the magistrates, determined foreign policy, and had a hand in almost every important domestic problem as well. (*See Reading No. 9B, C.*)

The Magistracies. The two consuls were the chief officers of state. Together with the praetors, they held the *imperium,* the right of command. An important area of their responsibility was always military. The *provinciae* to which the Senate assigned them were usually military tasks; only later did "province" come to designate a specific, dependent geographic area. The consuls presided over the centuriate assembly. In this capacity they exercised great influence over the election of their successors and other officials.

The dictatorship was an extraordinary office resorted to only in emergencies. The divided authority of the two consuls sometimes meant indecision and inaction. A dictator (chosen usually by the Senate, but sometimes by the assembly) temporarily took the place of both consuls. Symbolic of this were the twenty-four lictors assigned to him—double that of the consuls. The dictator was supposed to hold his post no longer than six months.

Praetors were, like the consuls, elected by the centuriate assembly. They too could command armies and ultimately, therefore, provinces as well. However, their chief function at Rome came to be associated with the law courts. The *praetor urbanus* supervised cases involving citizens, the *praetor peregrinus* those involving noncitizens. The *edicta* of the praetors, public proclamations of law and legal principle to be followed during the year, were important in the development of Roman law. At first (traditionally 367 B.C.) there was a single praetor. The second was added in the middle of the third century. More provinces meant more praetors. By the end of the Republic there were sixteen. To meet the growing need for magistrates the commands of consuls and praetors were often prorogued or continued. Proconsuls and propraetors (as they were called), ordinarily so designated by the Senate, were technically subordinate to their regularly elected successors.

The censorship was established during the fifth century. The two censors served about a year and a half, the only officials whose terms were for more than one year. They were elected usually about every five years. They took the census, assigning each citizen to his century (im-

portant militarily, politically, and for tax purposes). They
appointed and removed (for cause) members of the
cavalry and of the Senate. Later censors like Cato used
this power to influence morality, hence the developed
meaning of "censorship." By the middle Republic also,
the censor let important contracts for public works such
as roads and temples. (*See Reading No. 9B.*) For example, Appius Claudius Caecus, censor in 312 B.C., built
the first stage of the famed Appian way and also Rome's
first aqueduct, the Aqua Appia. The censors appointed
the *princeps senatus,* or first senator. In practice only
consulars were chosen censor.

Aediles from their original function (*see p. 22*) developed into supervisors of festivals and still later of the
great public games. By the late Republic they were expected to lavish personal funds on grand festivals. Men
like Caesar borrowed heavily to gain great popularity.
Aediles also supervised the forum and so exercised important judicial and police powers.

Quaestors were financial officials given general charge
of the treasury and public accounts. A quaestor was attached to each important commander for financial purposes. By the end of the Republic there were forty of
them.

A lesser office of some importance was that of military
tribune in the army, often the first elective post held by
an ambitious Roman. The tribunes were field-grade
officers. By the late Republic they were semiprofessionals.

The quaestorship, sometimes the aedileship, the praetorship, and the consulship were together called the
cursus honorum (course of honors). From the early Republic legislation (the *leges annales*) attempted to control the order in which these offices could be held, the
ages of candidates, and the period between offices or between repetitions of the same office. But the assemblies
always felt free to disregard or overrule these regulations
in specific instances.

It will have been noted that Roman society, institutions, and offices tended to adapt to new conditions. But
it was not always to be so. We shall find an increasing
inflexibility precisely at a time when rapid change made
unprecedented demands on Roman institutions and ways.

EXPANSION: CITY-STATE TO IMPERIAL POWER

Consolidation in Central Italy. Rome recovered rapidly from the Gallic disaster. A stone wall rose about the city, the remains of which (mistakenly called the "Servian" wall) may still be seen today. By the mid-fourth century Rome overshadowed the nearby Etruscan and Latin states. Members of the Latin league rebelled at least three times in the fifth and fourth centuries. The most serious struggle came about 340 B.C. The reasons for the revolt were, no doubt, that although by treaty equals in theory, in practice league members fought distant campaigns which served Roman purposes only.

Rome quelled the revolt by 338 B.C., and Roman leaders wisely effected a relatively liberal settlement. The Latin league was dissolved. A few Latin towns were absorbed into Rome; the names of the new citizens soon begin to appear on the lists of magistrates at Rome. Other Latin states remained autonomous, with their own officials and assemblies. These states, bound to Rome by treaty, were in effect isolated, for they could not enter into any other alliance. Each state had to furnish troops for the combined Roman-allied army, but no money tribute was exacted. Most Latin states had the right of trade (*commercium*) and of intermarriage (*connubium*) with Romans.

This relatively enlightened pattern became the system by which Rome dominated Italy. Two other features of the pattern also established by this date were important later. First, Rome laid down a policy of confiscating a portion (only) of the land of a conquered state which became Roman public land (*ager publicus*); secondly, Rome sometimes sent out citizen colonies to serve as military fortresses in newly acquired areas. Still it may be said that Rome dominated but did not tyrannize. This firm foundation would withstand even the stresses of a Hannibalic invasion.

The Samnite Wars. The Samnites, ethnically and linguistically related to the Romans, inhabited the rough areas east and south of Latium. One group of Samnites was now settled in Campania, largely displacing the Greeks and Etruscans of an earlier period. These Samnites (Oscans), relatively more civilized than their hill-country relatives, were often in alliance with Rome even against other Samnites. Indeed, the first Samnite war, about 343, was perhaps a Roman response to a plea from Oscans at Capua against the hill Samnites.

The second Samnite war (about 327 to 304 B.C. and probably the result of Roman expansion) was a severe test. In 321 B.C. a debacle at Caudine Forks saw a whole Roman army surrender. But within a few years the Romans forced the Samnites to ask for terms. The peace was not harsh. Rome acquired little land, but did profit strategically. Her colonies now had a strong hold on the Apulian coast, and her allies controlled the Campanian coast. The Samnites were hemmed in. Moreover, Rome was now allied with several Etruscan, Umbrian (Gallic), and Picentine states to the north.

In the third Samnite war (298-290 B.C.) a combination of all Rome's enemies in Italy—including, besides the Samnites. Gauls and Etruscans—very nearly put an end to Rome's predominance. The battle of Sentinum in Umbria (295 B.C.) was a desperate affair. Roman pertinacity plus spectacular generalship saved the day. Rome gained more territory, especially from the Gauls (the *ager Gallicus*), and more dependent allies. She now was indisputably the most powerful state in Italy. But a major hurdle remained.

The Pyrrhic Conflict. Greek Tarentum in South Italy resented the extension of Roman power. Roman colonies in strategic coastal sites threatened to encroach upon Tarentine sea trade. When a small Roman fleet appeared in the Tarentine gulf to support another Greek city, Thurii, against the Lucanians, the Tarentines declared that Rome had violated an old treaty. They attacked the fleet. Then they imported King Pyrrhus of

Epirus (modern Albania) and his army to take charge of the inevitable war.

The armies of the Hellenistic successors of Alexander the Great were the best in the world. Pyrrhus, a relative to Alexander's in-laws, was an adventurer-king who often had in his grasp rich prizes—as for example, twice the kingdom of Macedonia itself—but he lacked persistence. In Italy he soon showed that he really intended to dominate all Magna Graecia. But for the Romans, his army of about 25,000 men plus cavalry and elephants (and Greek allies) might have been able to manage the task.

In the first battle at Heraclea in 280 B.C., the Greek phalanx showed itself superior to the Roman legions in set battle. Still the Romans held their ground doggedly until Pyrrhus' elephants routed their screening cavalry. Perhaps Romans invented the king's reported remark that if he won another such battle he was lost, but it certainly was a "Pyrrhic" victory. The following year at Asculum in Apulia, Pyrrhus' elephants again decided a hard-fought battle. Now the king left the war in mid-cycle and went off to Syracuse to fight the Carthaginians. (*See Reading No. 4A.*)

In Sicily, Pyrrhus had initial success—which he failed to follow up. Meanwhile, the Romans began to recover their errant Italian allies (the Latins had never wavered). Urgent calls brought Pyrrhus back for a last battle against the Romans at Beneventum in 275 B.C. This time the Romans won. Pyrrhus returned to Epirus, soon invaded the Argolid, and was killed in street fighting in Argos. Rome now forced all of south Italy into familiar dependent alliance. Meanwhile she had been completing her subjugation of Etruria. By 265 B.C. Rome was in firm control of all Italy south of the Po valley.

The Struggle for the West: Carthage. Although some historians have seen a kind of inevitability in the struggle between Rome and Carthage, it could not easily have been foretold in 265 B.C. Carthage controlled much of the western Mediterranean including Sardinia and other islands uncomfortably close to Rome. But Carthaginian policy had not been notably expansionist for many years. Three times she had made alliances with Rome, most recently against Pyrrhus. (*See Reading No. 4A.*)

The first treaty, at the beginning of the Republic, amounted to a recognition of the new state. The second, in the mid-fourth century B.C., had recognized Rome's dominant position among the Latins. Rome in turn acknowledged Carthage's preëminence among her allies, and agreed not to infringe upon waters Carthage reserved for her own ships. None of these alliances bound the two states tightly together; and Rome's expansion had narrowed the buffer zone separating their vital interests. Still, no notable build-up of tensions occurred, and the spark which kindled the war must have been unexpected. However, each party seems to have taken up the challenge deliberately enough.

Carthage: The State. Carthage was founded by the city of Tyre probably in the first half of the eighth century B.C. She was located opposite the western tip of Sicily in North Africa near present-day Tunis on a well defended site. Carthage was a mercantile and trading city, but she also controlled much productive land in North Africa. She had a reputation, perhaps not altogether deserved, of treating her subjects shabbily.

The government of Carthage, an oligarchy of aristocracy and wealth, included a Senate, an inner group (Hundred) whose duties were partially judicial, and an assembly of all citizens. It elected the major officials, two Sufets and the generals. One person might combine both offices. By the time of the Punic (Latin for Phoenician) wars two political factions can be discerned, one conservative and closely oligarchical, the other expansionist and somewhat popular. The latter produced Rome's most bitter opponents like the Barcids, including the great Hannibal.

Carthage was immeasurably richer than Rome. Her navy was strong; Rome had practically no fleet at all. Carthage had fewer citizens and fewer dependable allies. She used mercenaries almost altogether, though a small body of citizen troops were usually held in reserve at home. (*See Reading No. 4C.*) Since Rome had few mercantile interests, there seemed little basis for contention. But there was Sicily, within sight of Roman-dominated Italy, and Rome now bore the responsibility for protecting the interest of Greek allies who did have commercial interests and who had for centuries opposed Carthaginian pretensions.

The First Punic War, 264-242 B.C. The incident which flared into war involved the control of Messina, on the straits between Sicily and Italy. The city had been seized by certain Mamertines (Campanian mercenaries) some time before. Syracuse's new king, Hiero, determined to reduce it. The Mamertines appealed for help both to Carthage and to Rome. Rome had shortly before reduced Rhegium when it had been similarly seized by Campanians and had summarily executed their leaders. However, Messina was the only city in eastern Sicily which had opposed Pyrrhus. The Romans did not want Carthaginian control of the straits. The prospect of a foothold in Sicily was tempting. Despite this, the Senate refused to recommend succor to the Mamertines; but one of the consuls, Appius Claudius Caudex, took the issue to the assembly and got a vote for intervention.

The Carthaginian army arrived first. However, the Punic commander was persuaded to evacuate, and Roman troops occupied the town. The Carthaginian general was called home and crucified, and the war was on. King Hiero, threatened with a stiff siege, became an ally, loyal to Rome for the next half century.

Rome Becomes a Sea Power. Carthaginian mercenaries did very well in Sicily early in the war, with the help of the fleet—which also raided the Italian coasts. Romans concluded that they too must build a fleet. In an early naval battle (260 B.C. off Messina at Mylae) the new Roman fleet defeated a Carthaginian contingent whose commander so scorned the Romans that he did not even put his vessels into fighting order. (*See Reading No. 4B.*) But there was to be no easy end to this war. The famous Hamilcar kept the Romans off balance in Sicily, and Carthaginian naval commanders partially recovered command of the sea.

Invasion of Africa (256-255 B.C.). The Romans decided to end this costly war by a daring invasion of Africa itself. A Roman expedition managed both to defeat an intercepting Carthaginian fleet and to land M. Atilius Regulus near Carthage with a sizable army. At this point the Carthaginians would have agreed to a reasonable peace, but Regulus' terms were harsh. Carthage hired new troops and a Spartan commander, Xanthippus, who defeated Regulus. A roman fleet picked up the remnants, but at sea a terrific storm overwhelmed nearly 200 Roman vessels. The following year a new Roman fleet was in turn lost to the elements. In 250 B.C. still another fleet was lost off western Sicily at Drepana through inept seamanship. (*See Reading No. 8B.*) By now Roman and allied casualties must have run to hundreds of thousands.

Victory and the Spoils. Rome was now exhausted in every way, but a fleet was an absolute necessity. Roman aristocrats brought their valuables as loans to the state; a new fleet of superior design took the water. After so many years this gamble paid off. An inferior Carthaginian force was destroyed. The fortified ports of western Sicily could not long hold out. Suddenly the long, bitter struggle was over. Carthage gave up Sicily and agreed to pay 3,200 talents over a period of ten years.

Carthaginian mercenaries had been made extravagant promises in the critical last months of the conflict. Defeat and default brought on an enervating mercenary war. When trouble arose also in Sardinia and troops were sent to that island to put down rebellious mercenaries there, Rome professed to be threatened. She arbitrarily seized Sardinia and Corsica (238 B.C.) and hiked the indemnity another 1,200 talents. The Carthaginians could only bear the humiliation. But Hamilcar Barca and his small son Hannibal swore undying enmity to Rome for this piece of unwarranted aggression.

The Second Punic War, 219-201 B.C. Carthage made an astonishingly quick recovery. This was in particular the work of Hamilcar, his son-in-law Hasdrubal, and his son Hannibal, in Spain. These men in succession controlled Carthaginian interests. They vastly extended the area of dominance and also uncovered rich deposits of gold and silver near New Carthage. The expansion northwards aroused the Greeks of Massilia, competitors of the Carthaginians in those waters. Rome was asked to intervene. A treaty was drawn up which established spheres of interest bounded by the Ebro river. But Rome also negotiated a treaty with Saguntum, south of the river. The right or wrong of the breach of peace which followed depends upon which treaty was drawn up first —a gap in our information which will probably never be filled. Nor does it matter much. By this time (219 B.C.) there is little doubt that Hannibal wanted war and that the Romans wanted to trim growing Carthaginian

power once again. Hannibal attacked Saguntum. Rome
sent an ultimatum which Carthage rejected. Another ti-
tanic struggle began.

Hannibal's Invasion of Italy. When war was formally
declared in 218 B.C., Hannibal determined on a strike
within Italy itself. He hoped for cooperation from Gauls
in the Po valley, recently subdued and partially displaced
by the Romans. With success he might hope to break
the allegiance of many Roman allies. Moreover, young
King Philip V of Macedonia might support Carthage.
The Romans had recently set up a military base in Illyria
(modern Yugoslavia), a move to stop piracy in the Adriatic. (*See Reading No. 11.*) This extension of Roman
power the king disliked.

A Roman army sent toward Spain hugged the coast
near Massilia, since the Roman commander felt that was
Hannibal's objective. But Hannibal moved into the in-
terior in order to cross the Rhone more easily with his
elephants and the two armies managed to miss each other.
Hannibal's forces crossed the Alps in the autumn, suffering from the assaults of intransigent tribesmen and the
weather. The Romans did not panic. They even sent their
army on into Spain.

Hannibal's Great Victories, 218-216 B.C. While
Hannibal recruited Gauls for his army, the consul
Tiberius Sempronius Longus quickly brought up his
troops from Sicily, where he had been staging for an
invasion of Africa. Longus let Hannibal trick him into
attacking early one wintry morning. Before his men had
breakfasted he sent them into the cold breast-deep water
of the flood-swelling Trebia river. An ambush drove most
of them back into the rising water where many drowned.
Only about 10,000 Roman infantrymen were able to
form line and cut straight through the Carthaginians and
Gauls to the security of a fortified city.

The following year the equally unwary Roman general
C. Flaminius lost most of his army to another of Hannibal's ambushes. (*See Reading No. 8B.*) Attacked while
marching along a fog-shrouded road by Lake Trasimene,
most Romans were slaughtered or drowned in the lake
before they learned what was going on.

Hannibal now marched south, ravaging Roman territory and working strenuously to break up the Roman

alliance system. In this crisis the Romans chose a dictator, Q. Fabius Maximus, who was given the surname Cunctator, the Delayer. He dogged Hannibal's army to prevent more widespread spoliation of the land and to make it more difficult for Hannibal to woo wavering allies. He hoped to trap the Punic army in unfamiliar terrain and very nearly did so. But Hannibal escaped. After six months Fabius resigned and consuls were chosen for the following year.

Rome's worst defeat ever came at Cannae in Apulia in this year, 216 B.C. The Romans had now combined the armies of both consuls and had a force numerically superior to Hannibal's. The Carthaginian army included some Gauls and a few Italians. Hannibal had superior cavalry. He picked his terrain carefully and "permitted" the Romans to bring him to battle. The Carthaginian center fell back before the Romans while Hannibal's cavalry was routing the Roman horse. The Carthaginian wings (his best infantry) held firm. When the cavalry returned to attack in the rear, the Romans were surrounded. Moreover, they were packed so tightly that most could not even get into the fray. Only about 10,000 escaped. The Romans reported their losses at 80,000. The actual number may have been less, but Cannae was a genuine debacle.

Some of Rome's most recently acquired allies in South Italy now went over to Hannibal, as did one older ally, Capua. Philip of Macedonia entered into alliance with Hannibal and promised aid. (See Reading No. 4D.) In Sicily King Hiero died, and Syracuse was soon aligned against Rome. But the Romans never even considered a negotiated peace. They called up old men and youths until new armies could be raised. (See Reading No. 4E.) It was these manpower reserves which really won this war of attrition.

Turn of the Tide. Hannibal stayed in Italy until 202 B.C., but accomplished nothing else of note. (See Reading No. 4F.) A critical point came in 207 B.C. when Hannibal's brother, Hasdrubal, with strong reinforcements, evaded the Romans in Spain and followed Hannibal's trail into Italy. But Romans annihilated this relieving army at the Metaurus river and informed Hannibal by throwing Hasdrubal's head into his camp.

Meanwhile Roman arms under young P. Cornelius
Scipio won Spain, completely excluding Carthaginians
by 206 B.C. The Romans had at last found a general.
They elected Scipio consul for 205 B.C. and assigned him
to an invasion of Africa. Scipio's successes there (204
and 203 B.C.) soon forced the Carthaginians to recall
Hannibal and his army. At Zama (202 B.C.) Scipio, with
the decisive aid of Numidian cavalry, finally defeated
Hannibal. Carthage sued for peace. The Romans of course
took Spain. They demanded 10,000 talents, to be paid
by installments. Carthage was reduced to control only of
the territory immediately surrounding the city. She could
make war in the future only with Roman permission.
Now surnamed Africanus, Scipio returned home to celebrate a grand triumphal procession. (*See Reading No.
15A.*)

The East: The Macedonian Wars. Rome had managed to keep Philip of Macedonia sufficiently involved
in Greece to keep him from fulfilling his promises to
Hannibal. He signed a separate peace in 205 B.C. But
Romans did not forget the stab in the back by the young
king. Moreover, members of the alliance they had formed
against Macedonia clamored for action. Attalus I of
Pergamum, among others, reported that Philip and
Antiochus III of Syria had formed an overwhelmingly
powerful combination which would first gobble up Egypt
and her possessions and then Rome itself. The Roman
Senate voted for war against Macedonia—but the people,
war weary, refused to second the vote in the assembly.
A little oratory, however, which argued that Rome would
have to fight in Greece with allies or alone face another
invasion of Italy, brought a declaration of war (200 B.C.).

Not until 198 B.C., when Rome at last assigned to the
war a competent general, Titus Quinctius Flamininus, did
this campaign pick up headway. For several years Rome
had been allied with the Aetolian League; Flamininus
persuaded the Achaean League also to join the alliance.
In a decisive battle at Cynoscephalae in 197 B.C. the
flexible legions penetrated the dangerous but rigid phalanx and decided the war. Philip was required only to
give up small territories in Greece and other areas, and
his fleet. He paid an indemnity of only 1,000 talents.

Flamininus was a genuine phihellene; he was also

young and a little naïve. Beset by the conflicting claims of allies he decided on an enlightened approach which he no doubt thought would solve Greece's problems for decades. At the Isthmian games in 196 B.C. he touched off a spectacular demonstration when he announced Rome's decision that all Greeks were to be free. (*See Reading No. 14A.*) This disappointed the Aetolians, who expected to profit from the war. The Romans apparently conceived an informal arrangement somewhat like the more formal alliance system in Italy. Greek states were to be autonomous but were not to start wars, and were expected to consult Rome in all serious problems. The Greeks hardly realized all this.

War with Antiochus III of Syria, 192-189 B.C. Antiochus (223-187 B.C.), a would-be Alexander, had raised Syria's power to the first rank. In a recent war with Ptolemaic Egypt he had won control of lower Syria. He next planned to seize Thrace and adjoining territories. A Roman embassy warned him to stay out of Europe, but Antiochus was cool to the gratuitous advice. When Hannibal fled Carthage, Antiochus gave him asylum. The Aetolians and other now disgruntled Greeks offered him alliance. He hoped, also, that in any showdown with the Romans Philip would assist him. When he occupied Thrace and appeared in Greece with an army, Rome declared war.

The Aetolians furnished only a fraction of the troops they had promised, and Antiochus himself brought only 10,000. Philip could see no good reason for joining this vigorous combination. A Roman army in 191 B.C. defeated the allies at Thermopylae. Late the following year at Magnesia in Asia Minor a Roman army under Lucius Scipio, brother to the great Africanus, who was Lucius' chief legate, defeated Antiochus. Again, as at Zama, cavalry furnished by an ally—this time by Eumenes II, now king of Pergamum—played a key role. In the struggle Antiochus made almost no use of Hannibal. The Carthaginian now fled to escape Roman vengeance and soon committed suicide. Lucius Scipio, of course, became Asiaticus.

Antiochus got severe terms. His holdings in Asia Minor the Romans bestowed on two allies, Pergamum and Rhodes. His elephants and navy were all but eliminated.

He was to pay to Rome 15,000 talents. He was soon killed while robbing a temple, no doubt in order to pay off. In Greece the Aetolians were punished and forced into dependent alliance. It is worthy of note that in neither of these eastern conflicts had the Romans taken any land. Roman imperialism thus far involved an extension of power and influence more than of land.

Third Macedonian War, 171-167 B.C. Philip of Macedonia was given exactly nothing for his aid during the Syrian war. Disputes with Greek states were invariably settled by Rome and just as invariably adversely to Macedonian interests. The king built up his treasury and his army for a possible later challenge to Rome. When he died in 179 B.C. his son Perseus became king. Romans had supported a younger son, Demetrius, who had become pro-Roman while a hostage. But Perseus had persuaded Philip to execute his half-brother for disloyalty.

No great cause was therefore needed to precipitate another conflict. When enemies of Perseus like Eumenes complained of the machinations of the Macedonian monarch, Romans were all too willing to listen. If ever Rome forced an unjustified war on an unwilling foe, this was it. Perseus seemed almost beaten from the beginning. He made little use of his full treasury to buy troops or to influence allies. Still he had the sympathy of many Greek states (*see Reading No. 14B*), and ultimately even of Rome's "friends" the Rhodians and Eumenes. The latter wanted Perseus curbed, not destroyed.

After three years of desultory and petty fighting, L. Aemilius Paullus, a tough general of the old school, defeated Perseus at Pydna in 168 B.C. A little later when the army complained over lack of the spoils to which Roman troops were becoming so accustomed, this general of high personal integrity (*see Reading No. 12A*) permitted his men to despoil scores of Illyrian towns which had opposed the Romans but surrendered. It was a sign of the times.

Perseus, halter about his neck, was led in the triumph at Rome. Still his kingdom was not absorbed by Rome. It was divided up into four separate, isolated republics. Greeks known to be anti-Roman were pretty generally punished. Many hundreds of relatives of leaders of the

Achaean league who were sympathizers of Perseus were taken hostage to Rome, among them the future historian Polybius.

Fourth Macedonian War, 149-148 B.C. It is not surprising that a false "son" of Perseus, Andriscus, was able to raise rebellion in divided and prostrate Macedonia. It is even less astonishing that L. Metellus "Macedonicus" and a Roman army quickly crushed the revolt. Now Macedonia was made a province of Rome. Achaeans, inflamed about the same time by the return of surviving hostages, joined in a "rebellion" and were similarly crushed. As an object lesson, Corinth, which was at the center of the struggle, was sacked and destroyed (146 B.C.) by the Roman commander L. Mummius. Greek cities outside Macedonia were subjected to varying treaties of dependence. The governor of Macedonia supervised affairs there. Only after the end of the Republic was the area formally designated the province of Achaea.

Third Punic War, 149-146 B.C. By terms of the peace of 201 B.C. Carthage could not make war without Roman approval. When, therefore, Masinissa of Numidia, ally of Rome, nibbled away on Carthaginian territory, the Carthaginians could do little but protest to Rome. On one occasion (153 B.C.) M. Porcius Cato led an investigative commission to Carthage. When the Carthaginians refused to submit trustingly in advance to the decision of the commission, Cato returned to Rome in high dudgeon, convinced that the Carthaginians were incorrigible. As every schoolboy knows, he thereafter continually demanded the destruction of Carthage. The actual declaration of war came when Carthage defiantly raised an army and actually made war on Numidia. Some scholars have suspected Rome of forcing the whole situation in order to reduce the growing pretensions of Numidia, but this attributes to Rome an unlikely wiliness.

The aristocratic party at Carthage adopted a peace-at-any-price policy. When the Roman army arrived on African soil, Carthage surrendered to Rome at her discretion. But after her people had given up their arms they were told to clear out of the city, since it was to be demolished. In desperation and with no more hope of final success than the Macedonians or the Achaeans had in Greece, the Carthaginians shut their gates and began to make more arms. One hope was that the army still in the field against Numidia would be able to accomplish some miracle. It was a forlorn hope.

The Roman army, mostly volunteers who hoped for quick spoils and glory, accomplished little at first. One junior officer was outstanding—P. Cornelius Scipio Aemilianus. The son of L. Aemilius Paullus, victor at Pydna, he had been adopted by the son of Scipio Africanus. He was elected consul for 146 B.C. though he was under age. He disciplined the army, took Carthage, and completely destroyed the city. Salt was sown on the site and it was cursed. (*See Reading No. 15C.*) Carthaginian territory became the Roman province of Africa.

Rome found other and formidable opponents in this period. Numantia in Spain, for example, had to be destroyed in 133 B.C. by Scipio Aemilianus. But no major power existed which might successfully challenge Rome. When the son of Antiochus III, Antiochus IV, occupied part of Egypt, a "friend" of Rome, he was forced out by the unauthorized bluff of an insolent ambassador. (*See Reading No. 14B.*) Roman power embraced the whole Mediterranean with a close grip.

— 6 —

A CENTURY OF CHANGE

Transformation: The Hub. The broad, swift, and irreversible transformations in thought, society, the economy, and the government make this century something of a turning point for all subsequent Roman history. We may perhaps find a key to all this significant change in one overriding fact: the Roman expansion into world power. The new situations, new encounters, new responsibilities demanded the service of Romans of all classes, particularly in the army. Roman and Italian soldiers served long years and in far and strange places. Some managed to enrich themselves; all were subjected to new influences to which they reacted in various ways. Roman magistrates, no longer the rulers of a small city only, became men of world-wide influence and authority. At home, the long series of successes, the income from booty and tribute brought prosperity. Roman and Italian cities grew turbulently. The influx of slaves, traders, ambassadors, and others made Rome a cosmopolitan center. Life there assumed a hustle and bustle previously unknown. Even the countryside was transformed. (*See Reading No. 9B.*) Everywhere men acquired new tastes and habits, new desires and drives.

Agricultural Change. The typical farm in early Rome was a small one. The farmer strove for self-sufficiency. He raised a few pigs, sheep, and fowl. He had a few trees of various sorts, and vines. A small grain crop provided him with bread. He was satisfied with a mud-and-wattle hut, a stall for his team of oxen, a fenced enclosure for the protection of his livestock. He had little to sell and purchased little, mostly iron tools and salt.

In the long wars, particularly the Hannibalic, Macedonian, and Syrian conflicts, the small property-holder fought on three continents. (*See Reading No. 7A.*) He was legally liable to sixteen years of service. This had usually meant summer training and occasional campaigning, but now he served whole years, sometimes far from home. If the Roman soldier's family could not somehow keep the farm in operation, it might be mortgaged and even lost. The discharged veteran would afterward find it hard to re-establish himself on the land. Even the simple tools, buildings, and livestock required were often beyond his ability to provide. Many historians have emphasized the competition of Sicilian wheat received as tribute as a cause of the impoverishment of the small farmer, but this idea is largely erroneous. The small farmer did not raise or need much of a cash crop. In any case only those farmers quite close to Rome would have been affected. It was not feasible to transport small quantities of surplus grain very many miles. Moreover, the needs of burgeoning Rome for other products would have more than offset the deleterious effects of a declining market for grain.

Perhaps another important reason why many small-holders left their farms is well expressed in the line from the popular song of World War I vintage: "How you gonna keep 'em down on the farm—after they've seen Paree?" The simple Roman who served in Greece or Asia developed a liking for luxuries and ways which the old hereditary acreage could never provide. Moreover, many such Romans profited in these second-century wars from booty or bonuses. These men could perhaps establish themselves in the city as small traders, craftsmen, or shopkeepers. Romans and Italians stayed in the cities because of economic opportunity or because the prospect of grubbing out a living on the little farm was drab in the face of urban attractions. There were religious festivals, public holidays, funeral games, and the theatre. The decrease in the numbers of small farmers was mostly gradual; the small independent producer emphatically did not disappear.

Rise of Large Farm Operations. To replace the small farms which were abandoned, sold, or lost, new and larger farms were organized by men who had the money to acquire and organize the land for production. One typical arrangement placed experienced freemen on the land on a tenant or sharecrop basis. Information about these tenant farms is scanty, but they were numerous.

Better known are the large, slave-operated plantations called *latifundia,* which developed in the most fertile areas. During much of the century slaves were cheap, for war captives there were in abundance. Land was available. It came in part from small farmers who migrated to the city. No doubt unscrupulous buyers drove a few smallholders from coveted plots. Roman aristocrats who made loans to the state in the late stages of the war against Hannibal later paid themselves back with Roman public land (*ager publicus*). In the south much excellent land seized from allies who had deserted to Hannibal was made available as public land to any who could pay the rental. These *latifundia,* most perhaps 100 to 200 acres in size, were capitalistic enterprises. Naturally they were expected to yield a profit. Consequently crops which would yield the most cash were emphasized: animals, olives, vines. It will be noted that livestock, olive oil, and wine have a high unit value and are all easily transported.

Decline of the Aristocracy. (*See Reading No. 6.*)
It is, perhaps, misleading to speak of the "decline" of the
aristocracy. They had actually increased their political
privileges and authority during the course of the Punic,
Macedonian, and Syrian wars. Only the Senate could
make and direct policy or effectively advise the magistrates. It controlled the growing treasury and the pro-
liferating provinces. (*See Reading No. 9B, C.*) Family
coalitions and class solidarity maintained firm and almost exclusive control over elections. However, the
social basis for the political power of the (landed)
aristocracy was distinctly weakening in the second century. The noble who owned *latifundia* might be richer
than his forebears (though he had much greater need
if he was to possess the new luxuries), but slaves did not
vote. The former clients of his family—or their offspring
—were no longer dependent upon him as patron. (*See
Reading No. 3C.*) Perhaps it would not have been apparent to the average Roman that the aristocratic oligarchy was in any danger, but the potential was there.
Only a crisis and a popular leader who could get votes of
the landless and patronless citizens in the popular assembly were needed to make it clear.

Growth of a Landless Proletariat. Not much is known
of the free tenant farmers and farm laborers. Those who
were former landowners or the sons of landowners cannot have been happy when they reflected on the great
benefits of Roman power which came to some Romans
only. Rural citizens such as these gave strong, sometimes
violent support to schemes for redistributing public land
after 133 B.C.

The new and growing city wage-earning class was more
diverse. Most were Roman citizens. But in a city where
change was a way of life, where old ties of patronage
broke down, this group was no longer intensely loyal to
the *mos maiorum* of which the nobles talked so much.
Especially after 146 B.C. the lower-class citizens increasingly found themselves in competition in the city with
slave laborers. How precarious was their economic position was not realized in prosperous times. But in a reces-
sion the slaves would not be laid off. The poor citizens
would have to bear the burden.

Even less attached to the old Roman ideals was the
growing number of lower-class citizens of foreign origin.

Most of these were former slaves. Rome was quite liberal in her treatment of freed slaves. They became voting citizens, retaining ties of clientage to the former master. Their votes were restricted to a single urban tribe. However, their descendants were not so restricted and could apparently be transferred to rural tribes where they held property. These freedmen-citizens had little understanding of or appreciation for Roman institutions.

The city poor were jammed into inadequate, slum-like housing. They were at the mercy of the erratic tides of economic fortune. They were cut off from any major benefit of the empire they had helped to create. They had the latent power to turn the Roman assembly of the people into a mob. When economic crisis came or when a demagogue inflamed them, they would do just that.

Rise of a Moneyed Class. This middle group was comprised of businessmen, contractors, bankers, moneylenders, traders, tax-contractors (*publicani*). The more wealthy were placed in the equestrian centuries in the census, along with the nobles. By the end of the century senators were no longer listed with them in the census, and they constituted a separate group. A few non-noble equestrians aspired to political careers and some few "new men" (singular, *novus homo*) even reached the consulship, ennobling themselves and their descendants. Most equestrians desired no more political power than was necessary to protect themselves and their activities. In the last century of the Republic they found themselves embroiled in politics. Their money made them important, and behind the political scene they played a role which cannot be fully assessed. (*See Reading No. 14E.*)

Just below the equestrians was a lower middle class of small businessmen, traders, shopowners, craftsmen-manufacturers, and the like. In the early Empire this group contributed to the stability of the times. However, neither segment of the moneyed class ever became large enough, vigorous enough, or prosperous enough generally to create an enduring social and economic well-being in Rome, Republic or Empire.

Cultural Changes in Rome. An outstanding characteristic of Rome was her willingness to accept outside ideas and practices and her ability to adapt them to her needs. Rome had long been influenced by Greeks, Etruscans, Carthaginians, and others. The second century B.C.

saw increasingly rapid and fundamental change. This, again, was due chiefly to Rome's expansion, to the new desires, the new values. These winds of change came in on two levels, material and intellectual. On both levels many Romans felt the new pressures pernicious and destructive. Rome changed, but not without struggle.

Materialism and Morals. A growing passion for material possessions was especially notable following the war against Syria. Thousands of Romans saw luxuries they had never dreamed of, and many of them gained the wherewithal to acquire a few of these. Jewels, finer clothing, pretty slaves of either sex, better food and slaves to cook it were much sought for in Rome. The old virtues-of-necessity, austerity and abstinence, gave way to new desires for ease and pleasure. (*See Reading No. 12.*) The relaxed Greek attitude toward sexual morals appealed to young upper-class Romans, and even homosexualism was reported among them. (*See Reading No. 7B.*)

Conservative Romans, especially older ones, apprehended that the new standards threatened not merely the integrity of a few individuals, but the state itself. (*See Reading No. 8.*) Heading the reaction to this "foreign subversion" was Marcus Porcius Cato (234-148 B.C.), a doughty and indefatigable foe indeed. (*See Readings No. 8B and 15B.*) As censor in 184 B.C. Cato assessed at ten times their market value expensive clothing, jewels, vehicles, and young slaves valued (no doubt) for their sex appeal. He did not hesitate to expel from the Senate a member of the highest nobility, Lucius Quinctius Flamininus, brother of the victor at Pydna, for a lapse of morals and integrity. All his life he heaped caustic criticism on the "Greeklings," superficial philhellenes. Yet, he owned *latifundia,* and the oldest extant piece of Latin prose is his *De Agricultura,* which tells how to select land for such an operation, how to stock and run it. Moreover, Cato knew Greek (although he pretended he did not) and was conversant with at least some works of Greek literature.

Religious Innovations. The great flood of oriental religions was a phenomenon chiefly of the first century B.C. and the early Empire. Innovations came also in the second century, and the Roman reaction to them is most instructive. In the anxious days when Hannibal stalked Italy many strange religious practices cropped up in Rome. (*See Reading No. 4F.*) In 210 B.C. a praetor attempted to eliminate them. Before the end of the war, Roman nobles themselves brought in a new deity at the command of the Sibylline books. The new goddess was Cybele, the Magna Mater. Her image was brought from Pessinus in Asia Minor, center of the ancient cult. The Romans then built her a temple within the city. Romans were repelled by the noisy processions in her Spring festival when would-be priests emasculated themselves. It was decreed that Roman citizens could not be priests to her. Nevertheless the Megalensian games, devoted to her, became the most important spring festival. Her rites were always somehow associated with the upper aristocracy in the Republic.

A second religious movement which the Romans disliked and even feared was the rites of Dionysus (Latin Bacchus or Liber), god of wine. The Senate heard that these nocturnal and mysterious rites were spreading in Italy and that devotees were debauching young men. The Romans chose to view the movement as a threat to the state. The oath of secrecy they called a conspiracy. The Senate launched a grand witch hunt; some thousands of persons ultimately were executed. Most of them were probably guilty of nothing more than a degree of immorality. This senatorial decree of 186 B.C. has been preserved and is the oldest Latin inscription of any length. The decree is also perhaps the earliest instance in which the Roman Senate presumed to legislate for all Italy.

The Romans and Greek Philosophy. A book-burning in 181 B.C. illustrates interestingly the conservative attitude toward un-Roman philosophical views. Books said to have been dug up on the Janiculan hill across the Tiber dealt, it was asserted, with Pythagorean philosophy. Politically, some Pythagoreans are known to have held reformist views. A praetor declared the books subversive of religion, and by decree of the Senate they were burned. The whole incident was conceivably a hoax, but a solemn warning to any Romans who—like the poet Ennius—held Pythagorean views.

Cato's contempt for Greek philosophy is well known. His influence is to be seen in the banishment of philosophers and rhetoricians from Rome in 161 B.C. and in the abrupt treatment given Carneades, Diogenes, and Critolaus in 154 B.C. Carneades, head of the Academy and a skeptic, lectured twice on justice. This concept the Romans understood as synonymous with law and tradition. Carneades' first lecture warmed the cockles of their hearts. But on the next day he completely demolished his own previous arguments! This procedure brought the *mos maiorum* into question, a serious matter. It is, perhaps, illuminating to reflect that philosophical rationalism in an atmosphere of change must have produced an impact somewhat like that of the Sophists in fifth-century Athens.

Hellenistic Intellectualism at Rome. Latinized Greek drama was first produced at Rome in 240 B.C. Plautus (254-184 B.C.), the first important Roman dramatist, was already doing his best work at the turn of the century. (*See Readings No. 7B and 8D.*) The intensive Hellenic influence of the second century produced plays more closely imitative of Greek authors like Menander, both in form and content. Such were the works of Terence (c. 195-159 B.C.), more polished in form, less racy in content than those of Plautus. (*See Reading No. 7C.*) These authors found it expedient to keep the plots, characters, and scenes Greek. No Roman matron or paterfamilias was portrayed in any questionable situation. Conservatives apparently staged no strong attack on the theatre. Still there must have been opposition, for attempts in mid-century to build a permanent theatre were thwarted, and not for a hundred years did Pompey give to Rome her first stone theatre.

The "Scipionic Circle." The new philhellenism may be credited in part to the use of Greek tutors and to the reading of Greek authors. There arose in Rome an intellectual group whose aim was to synthesize the new Greek learning with the best of Roman ideas and traditions. (*See Reading No. 7C.*) Since the great Scipio Aemilianus was at the center of the group, it has been called the "Scipionic Circle." It is uncritical to associate with this group all intellectuals in Rome, as is often done. A most important Greek member of the group was the historian Polybius (c. 208-126 B.C.), Book Six of whose history is the most important source of information about the constitution of the middle Roman Republic. Son of an important Achaean League official, Polybius was brought to Rome as a hostage in 167 B.C. He was tutor to Aemilianus and often his companion in his later career. Probably no less influential was Panaetius (c. 180-111 B.C.), a Stoic philosopher of Rhodes who was associated with Scipio in Rome about the third quarter of the century. Panaetius created a Romanized Stoicism. Not only was it palatable to Romans; it dovetailed so well with Roman views of duty and the state that it has been called more Roman than Stoic.

Other important members of this "circle" were Laelius, close friend of Scipio, and Lucilius (c. 180-103 B.C.), chief formulator of satire as a separate literary genre— the one category of literature in which Romans exercised considerable originality.

Basic Conservatism Unchanged. Old Cato and Scipio Aemilianus were not really in basic disagreement. (*See Reading No. 8C.*) Neither wanted to see the integrity of the Roman people or the Roman constitution upset. They did not see eye to eye as to the dangers which might lie in an intellectual philhellenism. Men like Scipio admired the great Hellenic achievements of the past. But all upper-class Romans rejected out of hand the social and economic implications of more recent Greek internal strife. Class struggle in Hellenistic Greece brought frequent demands for cancellation of debts and redistribution of the property of the wealthy. No Roman politician wanted to see similar turmoil in Italy.

Until the Gracchi, then, the old conservative traditions remained firmly entrenched. But the changes here discussed, new material emphasis, changing morals, fluid class situation, the large element of foreign stock at Rome, and above all expansion into empire (though we still refer to it as the Republic) which brought great opportunity monopolized by the oligarchy—all these meant that the stability of mid-century was more apparent than real. The political structure and the oligarchy itself had grown more rigid instead of adapting itself to the changed world. (An exception was the judicial and legal system. *See Reading No. 10.*) A reckoning was coming.

A CENTURY OF CONFLICT:
THE INITIAL PHASE

Boom and Bust in Rome. Through most of the second century Rome grew rapidly. The swelling population required manifold more supplies which must be brought to the city by boat up the Tiber or by land transport. The number of specialized craftsmen and tradesmen multiplied. There were metal workers of various sorts, carpenters and woodworkers, leatherworkers, shoemakers, weavers, fullers, dyers, masons, brickmakers, tile makers, potters. Public building activity reached a peak in the years immediately following the series of wars ending in 146 B.C. Several temples were built, some in elaborate compounds or squares. Rome's largest aqueduct, the Aqua Marcia, was constructed to meet the greater need for water. The general prosperity plus citizens' shares of booty from Corinth or Carthage made possible accelerated private building as well. The rest of the world might not fare so well, but Rome was something of a boom town.

After about 140 B.C., however, the economic pace slackened. The extraordinary income ceased. Public construction, so far as can be determined, fell off to almost nothing. Indeed, far from having surpluses, the Roman treasury was forced to support a series of relatively small-scale and unprofitable wars against semibarbarous tribesmen in Spain, Illyria, and Macedonia, and against slaves in Sicily. Tribute from those provinces fell off. There was no longer a stream of newly discharged and often well-heeled veterans to bolster the economy. The supply of slaves, however, continued to be plentiful. It was about this time that increased use of slaves in the city industries and crafts began to bear heavily upon the vulnerable free laborers at Rome. The effects of a slackening economy probably were scarcely felt by the upper classes. But there were misery and unemployment for much of Rome's economic substratum.

Impact of Slave Rebellion. Rome's first serious slave war compounded the economic difficulties for the lower classes in that city. The outbreak occurred on the island of Sicily. It assumed serious proportions in 135 B.C. when one Eunus, a man of remarkable ability and something of a priest, prophet, and political visionary, organized the slaves into a formidable army. The rebellion lasted several years. Ultimately a full-scale consular army was needed to suppress it.

Rome had become dependent upon grain brought in by way of tribute from Sicily. Her market required not only the tribute-tithe of Sicilian wheat; additional purchases were regularly made there. Sicily may have furnished half the grain consumed in Rome. In the city, therefore, the slave war meant a severe shortage of grain. The usual speculation in the market no doubt forced prices up even more precipitately. Rome's poor, already plagued with unemployment, were faced with sharply rising prices for bread, which was the chief item of their diet. The solution to this difficulty, one would expect, would be to import quantities of grain from elsewhere in the Mediterranean. However, a shortage of grain plagued the eastern Mediterranean also. There is evidence of a rapid and continuing rise of prices there from about 140 to about 127 B.C. This was partly due to piracy; there were pirates even about Italy. Rome had not yet recognized her responsibility to keep this scourge under control. States like Rhodes, weakened by Roman policies in the Aegean, could no longer assume the task. This urban crisis pointed up the dangers which had been long developing. Too many lower-class Romans had for one reason or another come to the city. Too little grain was produced in central Italy. The new large capitalistic farm operators found it unprofitable.

Another related and quite serious problem involved the army. Despite the lowering of property requirements Rome was having difficulty finding an adequate number of property-holders to man the legions. When Scipio Aemilianus prepared for the siege and destruction of

Numantia (135-133 B.C.), he had to ask for "volunteers" from Rome's overseas allies. Many Romans felt that if only the class of small farmers could be restored, several of these problems would solve themselves. Rome would then need less grain. Fewer unemployed would roam the streets. More propertied citizens would be available for army duty. These long-range developments and the immediate and acute urban crisis help to explain the tribuneship of Tiberius Gracchus.

Tiberius Gracchus: The Background of Political Factions. *Pietas*—a sense of duty to gods, family, and country—was a most important concept to Romans. In the second century B.C. these ties, though weakening, were still strong. Family ties and connections between families affected both the form and function of Roman politics. These family groups or factions were not really political parties. The lineup of the factions was not rigid. Nevertheless, they played an especially important role in the last two centuries of the Republic.

Major family factions about the time of the war with Hannibal were the Fabians, Scipionians, and Claudians. (*See Reading No. 6C.*) The Fabians were centered about the Fabius gens. Old Cato was sponsored by a family in this faction, and his basic conservatism illustrates its general outlook. However, this group had virtually disappeared by 133 B.C. The Scipionians (Scipionii, Aemilii, Livii, and others) were strongly attached to the customs and traditions of old Rome. They were in some degree philhellenist and were willing to learn from Greek ideas and experience. (*See pp. 46f.*) Since the popularity of the Scipionians was closely related to their success in war, some members of the faction tended toward imperialism. The third major family faction was the Claudian. Leaders of this faction are difficult to classify. They were not notably successful generals. On the domestic front, however, they often sought popular favor. For example, they supported and carried out colonization schemes. Through their efforts large numbers of Romans were settled in the Po valley, particularly in the period just before the Hannibalic war and again in the two decades before the war with Perseus. It should be added that Claudians were at times inclined to give favored treatment to citizens; Latins and Italians did not always fare so well.

The Sempronii (the gens name of the Gracchi) were long-standing partners in the Claudian faction. The father of the Gracchi, Tiberius Sempronius Gracchus, was a political enemy of known Scipionians. It is true that he married the daughter of Scipio Africanus after Scipio was dead. And the younger Scipio married Sempronia, sister of the Gracchi. These alliances may represent one of the several known efforts to reconcile factions or at least cross party lines. Still, the identification of Tiberius and Gaius Gracchus with the Claudian faction is definite. The future tribune of 133 B.C. was married to a daughter of the Claudian leader, Appius Claudius. His younger brother Gaius married the daughter of P. Licinius Crassus Mucianus (that is, adopted from the Mucius family), another leading Claudian.

The father of the Gracchi was twice consul (177 and 163 B.C.), and censor in 169 B.C. He was governor of Spain and of Corsica and Sardinia. Twice he was legate or roving ambassador in the eastern Mediterranean. In the Roman style he had made himself patron at Rome of provincial and foreign interests from Spain to Asia Minor. When young Tiberius and Gaius in their turn served in Spain and Sardinia and when they took a special interest in the new province of Asia (formerly the Kingdom of Pergamum), there was nothing accidental about it. The system of patronship was hereditary; the family had a strong sense of responsibility toward these areas. (*See Reading No. 3C.*) When young Tiberius was elected tribune, he had strong support from family and faction. Members of the faction continued to support the operation of his agrarian law even after his death.

The Agrarian Law of Tiberius Gracchus, 133 B.C. Soon after his accession to office December 10, 134 B.C., Tiberius Gracchus came forward with his controversial law for distribution of certain public lands. As we have seen, he was motivated by the economic crisis at Rome and by his concern for the declining numbers of Roman smallholders eligible for army service. He did not consider himself in any sense a revolutionary. The agrarian law itself was patterned upon earlier legislation long disregarded.

Ancient writers suggest that Tiberius acted with some partisan bitterness because a vote of the Senate had overturned a treaty he had concluded in Spain as quaestor to an inept governor. This is properly discounted by modern historians, but a challenge to the family patronage was no light thing. There is no reason to doubt Tiberius' idealism. However, Tiberius, in common with many idealists, considered himself so unalterably right that anyone who opposed him must be evil. Similarly, he was impatient with any procedures, time-hallowed or not, which obstructed his aims. With absolute confidence and complete dedication to public welfare—but with no little obstinacy—he ushered Rome into a constitutional crisis which was not to be completely resolved until the Republic had been smothered under a blanket of imperial authority.

Tiberius' agrarian law did not involve private property at all, only Roman public land (*ager publicus*). All such land in excess of 500 *iugera* (about 300 acres) held by a single individual was to be repossessed by the state. (An additional 500 *iugera* could be held by men who had two sons.) The land recovered from them (and from unauthorized possessors) was to be distributed in small lots to Roman poor. In usual fashion the opposition found a tribune, Octavius, to veto this proposed legislation. Tiberius, outraged, staged an unprecedented recall election, declared Octavius deposed, and had him dragged from his station. A friend was elected to replace him. Then the law was passed. A commission of three—Tiberius himself, his twenty-year-old brother Gaius, and his father-in-law, Appius Claudius—began to administer the program.

Work of the Agrarian Commission. The commission encountered very knotty problems. The three surely expected opposition from aristocratic and equestrian Romans holding large blocs of public land. But Italians also held much of this land. In fact, the commission seems to have concentrated on public land confiscated since the Hannibalic war. Large sections declared to be Roman had never actually been taken over by the state. Thorough surveys had never been made; land had changed hands, the buyers not realizing titles were questionable. Buildings, vineyards, olive orchards had been reared at much expense. The storm of protest must have astonished many Romans. Italians resented bitterly this and succeeding agrarian legislation of the Romans. Nothing made them feel more strongly their inferior status.

Another difficulty was that the Romans eligible for land allotments had not the resources to build buildings and buy tools, oxen, and other livestock. The Senate would not help. Indeed, it would not even provide an expense allowance for the commission. This need led Tiberius to other moves of grave constitutional implications. Through his father's connections (no doubt) he heard of the death of Attalus III, King of Pergamum, and of his will—which bequeathed kingdom and treasury to Rome. In the tribal assembly Tiberius proposed to make use of the treasury for his program. Moreover, he declared that the assembly (under his leadership, of course) would administer the kingdom's affairs and settle Pergamum as a Roman province.

These proceedings seemed equitable to Tiberius. But to the opposition nobles Tiberius was encroaching on senatorial authority. The Senate had long controlled all affairs relating to the provinces. It had controlled the public purse strings. Tiberius had already shown his contempt, they felt, for the Roman constitution when he had a properly elected tribune thrown out. When further Tiberius now announced himself a candidate for re-election, many senators considered the action illegal and indeed subversive of the Roman state.

Assassination of Tiberius; Repression. At the elections, feeling ran high. There was disorder. Some senators declared before the Senate that they had heard that Tiberius intended to make himself king or a tyrant of the Greek sort. Excited aristocrats demanded that the consul act to stop the disorder and prevent Tiberius' "illegal" actions. The consul, Q. Mucius Scaevola, was a Claudian and naturally refused to act. Scipio Nasica, the *pontifex maximus,* called for all who would preserve the constitution to follow him. Senators and retainers seized clubs and stones, charged into the crowd around Tiberius, and killed him and several hundred of his supporters. Tiberius' body was thrown into the Tiber.

A period of repression followed. Some followers of Gracchus were killed. Blossius, the Stoic adviser of Tiberius, was questioned and released. He fled to the former Kingdom of Pergamum. With the pretender,

Aristonicus, he roused the natives to rebellion, proclaiming plans for a utopian "sun-state." Both were eventually killed. By 130 Rome was in firm control. The new province was called Asia.

The agrarian commission continued to function. Crassus was appointed in Tiberius' place to serve with his son-in-law Gaius Gracchus and Claudius. In 129 B.C. indignant Italians approached Scipio Aemilianus (back from Spain) to ask him to intervene. Scipio got the Senate to curtail the judicial authority of the commission. It continued to operate, but on a much restricted basis. The lower classes in Rome were incensed at Scipio. When he was found mysteriously dead in bed, there was no investigation. The most eminent man of his age was not even given a public funeral. Scipio Nasica found it advisable to leave Rome and shortly after died a virtual exile.

It is not possible to assess the material results of the Gracchan law. Census figures show a large increase in citizen-rolls between 131 and 126 B.C., but these are subject to various interpretations. It is certain that the concentration of lower-class citizens in Rome continued. No adequate supply of smallholders was created to man the armies. But the system of handling the public land was at least partially regularized. Some thousands of Romans were surely settled on the land. More important for the city poor was the end of the Spanish war and of the slave war in Sicily. Bread was cheaper again, although it appears that grain prices remained abnormally high.

Changed "Party" Structure. One of the more important, if completely unintended results of the work of Tiberius Gracchus was the sharp division of the ruling class during the last century of the Republic. (*See Reading No. 13.*) *Populares* were leaders who like Tiberius appealed to the lower classes for support for a popular program. Like Tiberius they functioned chiefly through the tribuneship and the assembly of the tribes. They therefore opposed senatorial control, especially of armies, the treasury, and the provinces. However, the popular leaders were themselves senators and aristocrats—or even patricians. They represented a large minority of all the nobles. Their opponents, *optimates,* they called themselves, were

champions of the oligarchical system which functioned
in and through the Senate.

It is not proper to equate the popular movement with
democracy, though popularis leaders like the tribune C.
Papirius Carbo sponsored democratic legislation. Carbo's
law (131 or 130 B.C.), one of three similar measures,
introduced the secret ballot into assemblies for voting
on legislation. The Roman assemblies could not possibly
meet frequently enough—Roman citizens were settled all
over Italy—to function in democratic fashion. The tendency of this movement, whether Tiberius Gracchus
realized it or not, was toward the one-man rule which
finally developed.

Neither is it proper to equate the optimate cause with
any genuine form of republic. The *optimates* really stood
for a very restricted oligarchy. There were those like
Cicero (*see p. 73*) who advocated a broadened oligarchy.
But in the bitter struggle most leaders were forced to one
extreme or the other. Middle-of-the-roaders were squeezed
out. The expanding power of Rome called for an expansion of benefits and responsibilities. Failure of the nar-
rowly exclusive ruling class to provide for this meant
that the overthrow of the "Republic" was very nearly
inevitable.

The Tribuneships of Gaius Gracchus. The younger
Gracchus was elected tribune for 123 B.C. just after a
tour of duty as quaestor in Sardinia. The preceding dec-
ade had produced no great changes in Roman affairs. The
secret ballot was now used in every phase of the assembly's activities. It had been enacted into law that a
tribune could succeed himself. The old Latin colony
of Fregellae had rebelled and been destroyed (125 B.C.)
probably because of increasing resentment by Latins and
Italians of their inferior status. Fulvius Flaccus, consul
in 125, had tried without success to obtain the citizenship for Latins and Italians. The economic situation in
the city may have worsened again. We hear of a locust
plague in North Africa and destruction of crops. One of
the consuls of 123 B.C. was given a command against
pirates which infested the Balearic isles. Grain prices
generally were still high. The miserable poor at Rome
were as numerous as ever.

Gaius Gracchus was more the politician than Tiberius,

actuated more by ambition, less by impatient idealism.
He depended less on the support of his faction than on
the reputation Tiberius had established. Naturally enough
he hated the oligarchs who had murdered his brother.
In the two years of his tribuneship (123 and 122 B.C.) he
tried to destroy those *optimates* who had a stranglehold
on the government.

Some of his earlier measures seem primarily to have
been intended to assure Romans that he would follow in
the footsteps of his brother. He re-enacted the agrarian
law, for example, perhaps to restore full power to the
existing commission. Other proposals demonstrated his
approval of Tiberius' acts and his condemnation of the
arbitrary executions following his brother's assassination.
A law against bribery of jurors reflected on the integrity
of senators. Another piece of legislation reduced the
power of the Senate to assign specific provinces to particular magistrates.

Major Legislation of Gaius Gracchus. Gaius passed a
law which subsidized grain for the Roman poor. The price
he set was perhaps no less than earlier stable prices, but
much less than the going rate. To maintain a stable food
supply he built extensive granaries. A colonization scheme
was devised for the "better sort" of citizens, perhaps
those in the lower middle class. By it he sent colonies to
commercially important sites such as Tarentum in Italy
and Carthage in Africa. The allotments of 200 *iugera*
(about 120 acres) could only have been operated by
tenants or slaves.

Most significant were the efforts of Gaius to gain the
support of the richer equestrians while at the same time
putting them at odds with the Senate. He set up for the
new province of Asia the system of tax-farming by
publicani, a lucrative source of income for them. He arranged for equestrians to man the important extortion
court. This permanent court had been set up in 149 B.C.
by the Senate to control provincial governors. Through
this court it was at least possible that outraged provincials
might obtain redress. Gracchus' law forced provincial
governors to defer to powerful equestrians and their
agents in the provinces. (*See Reading No. 14E.*) Unfortunately, as it developed, the provincials needed protection against publicans and money lenders at least as
badly as against governors. The new jurors were not

subject to prosecution for bribery, for Gracchus did not revise his earlier law. He probably felt that these jurors needed to be protected from the harassment of political prosecutions so characteristic of the last two centuries of the Republic.

The Counterproposals of Livius Drusus. Gaius Gracchus' attacks had weakened the authority of the Senate. At length most senators agreed to support Livius Drusus in a counter-program. Drusus was a Scipionian with Italian connections. He was no reactionary, and there is no good reason to doubt his sincerity. As tribune with Gracchus in 122 B.C. Drusus announced his program. There was a colonization scheme. Allotments already received from the public land were to be free of rent; this meant in effect that the Senate accepted what had been done under the Gracchan land laws. It also made the land private property and salable. Gaius' laws had again aroused the Italians to violent protest. Implicit in Drusus' proposals was the assurance to them that the distributions in the Gracchan fashion would cease. He also proposed that Latins should not be subject to scourging in the army (an alternative to full citizenship).

Gracchus' Defeat and Demise. In his re-election campaign Gracchus felt it necessary to calm the fears of the Latins and Italians. He proposed to give them full citizenship. Such a proposal was feared by the Senate and disliked by lower-class citizens. Senators thought all the new voters would support Gracchus. The Roman poor did not want Italians crowding into Rome for the public festivals. The *optimates* carried on a propaganda campaign against Gaius, especially harping on the dangers of a revived Carthage. Gracchus was defeated in his bid for a third tribuneship. For the remainder of his last year as tribune he was an extinct volcano.

One of the consuls for 121 B.C., Lucius Opimius, was an avowed enemy of Gracchus. Gracchus and Flaccus with close supporters attempted to prevent any annulment of Gracchus' laws. In a public gathering (*contio*) called to discuss possible repeal of one law some of Gracchus' men murdered a herald of the consul. Opimius and his supporters made the murder a *cause célèbre*. For Gracchus and Flaccus it meant danger of exile or perhaps even execution.

The consul was empowered by the Senate through a

"final" decree (*senatus consultum ultimum*) to take extraordinary action. This was perhaps the first use of this decree, which established a kind of martial law. The following day Gracchus and Flaccus ignored a command to appear before the consul and barricaded themselves atop the Aventine. They attempted to negotiate, but Opimius would have nothing short of surrender. Finally troops stormed the barricades. Gracchus, Flaccus, and most of their close supporters were slain. Some were executed without trial or right of appeal in the investigative vendetta following.

Opimius felt he had saved the state. The Gracchi were gone. He built a temple to Concordia, imitating the men who ended the great discord in 367 B.C. In fact this harsh repression only embittered many Romans. Enactments such as the Final Decree were to be foci of partisan strife to the end of the Republic. However, the victorious reactionaries did not dare to wipe out all the Gracchan acts. The colonies remained; the land distributions were left untouched. The equestrians retained their control of the extortion court juries. An uneasy peace descended. The economic depression passed. But things would never be the same.

— 8 —

MARIUS TO SULLA, 120-80 B.C.

Jugurtha, the Numidian War, and Roman Politics. The assassination of Gaius Gracchus brought no real settlement of issues. As early as 120 B.C. a tribune, P. Decius, denounced Opimius' inquisition and the illegal executions without trial. Gaius Marius, best known popular leader following the Gracchi, made his political debut as tribune in the following year (119 B.C.). He defied both consuls and Senate and passed some sort of measure which made it more difficult to tamper with voters at the elections. The repression would not last; more trouble would come, in every major issue.

The next severe outbreak of partisan strife came over the conduct of the Jugurthan war (111-105 B.C.). Jugurtha was an adoptive grandson of Massinissa, King of Numidia, who was an ally of Rome from the last years of the Hannibalic war until his death at an advanced age in 148 B.C. Micipsa, his son, after a long reign also, at his death (118 B.C.) divided the kingdom among his two sons and an adopted son, Jugurtha. The latter had served in Spain under Scipio Aemilianus (the Scipios played the role of patrons at Rome to the kingdom), and it was perhaps due to his commendation that Jugurtha had been adopted. Intensely ambitious, Jugurtha eliminated both of his foster brothers. Appeals were made to Rome. Soon popular leaders accused *optimates* involved in attempts at settlement of taking bribes from Jugurtha. The chief source of information is Sallust, a Caesarian of the middle first century, whose *Jugurthan War* portrays the optimate senators as venal and vacillating. No doubt Sallust exaggerated; however, he also had access to excellent information. One can imagine the arguments on the question of Rome's right to intervene in the internal affairs of an overseas allied state.

Jugurtha was not willing to accept any real curb. Also he alienated the Roman middle class by killing some Italian traders in a siege of Cirta, 112 B.C. Popular leaders demanded and got war. But the army conscripted was inefficient, the general was incompetent, and Jugurtha got an easy peace. Perhaps, as the *populares* shouted, there was more bribery. After a tremendous row in Rome the war was renewed under Q. Caecilius Metellus (consul 109 B.C.). Gaius Marius was a legate on his staff. Metellus quickly gained victories over the forces of Jugurtha, but found himself unable to bring the war to a quick conclusion.

Marius Given African Command. Marius believed he could better command the war. Moreover, he hoped that he might as a "new man" achieve the consulship. Against the wishes of Metellus, who was probably family patron as well as commanding officer of Marius, the latter returned to Rome and in a mud-slinging campaign gained both the consulship (107 B.C.) and by special vote of the tribal assembly the command of the Numidian war. Metellus went home and, surprisingly, received a hero's welcome—and the face-saving name Numidicus. Marius was successful in Africa, but the war dragged on. Jugurtha was ultimately captured through the machinations of a lieuenant of Marius named L. Cornelius Sulla, and Numidia became a province of Rome.

A New Command: The Northern Invaders. During the last years of the Jugurthan war Rome faced a much more serious military threat at home. Migrating Germanic tribes, chiefly the Cimbri and Teutoni, entered the area of present-day France. To protect the new province of Narbonensian Gaul (centered about Massilia, near modern Marseilles, acquired in 118 B.C.), large armies were sent north. A series of defeats was capped by a debacle at Arausio (105 B.C.) in which an estimated 80,000 Romans perished. An optimate pro-consul, Q. Servilius Caepio, had stubbornly refused to cooperate with his technical superior, the consul Cn. Mallius, who like Marius was a "new man." At Arausio the Gauls had therefore been able to destroy the two armies in separate battles a short distance apart.

Caepio during his consulship in 106 B.C. had attempted to reverse the law of Gaius Gracchus which had put the extortion courts into equestrian hands. Worse, treasure he had taken at the Gallic town of Tolosa mysteriously disappeared on its way to Rome. And now he was held responsible for Arausio. He seemed personally to epitomize the faults which the *populares* saw in the *optimates:* greed, arrogance, incompetence.

In 103 B.C. a popular tribune, L. Appuleius Saturninus, haled Caepio before a special court. He and others were convicted and exiled. Meanwhile, by popular demand, Marius received the command in the north (104 B.C.). In 102 and 101 B.C., in two great battles, he crushed the invaders at Aquae Sextiae and in the Po valley. Meanwhile, he held his second to sixth consulships in successive years, 104-100 B.C. This was contrary to law but possibly in this crisis approved by the Senate, for there must be no question of supreme command.

Marius' Army Reforms. Marius reformed army organization, tactics, and weaponry. More significantly, he recruited his men from the unpropertied classes. A military man more than a politician, he probably found that the old system simply did not yield enough soldiers. The change was nevertheless important politically. These new soldiers tended to become professionals; for them there was no better economic opportunity. Their fortunes, both in the army and on their discharge, depended on their leader.

Marius did take care of his men. After the wars, jealous *optimates* would do nothing for his veterans. Consequently, Marius allied himself with Saturninus, who arranged land grants as discharge bonuses for Marius' troops. The ballots of the veterans themselves weighed heavily in the voting, as they had, no doubt, in the annual re-election of Marius himself. Thus, almost unwittingly, Marius blazed the path for ambitious Roman commanders of the later Republic. Hereafter, political preferment would come most easily through an important command and an emergency army of lower-class troops sworn by personal oath to their commander. (*See Reading No. 9E.*) It was a fatal pattern, but the Roman system of giving nearly unchecked power to commanders made it almost an inevitable one.

Fall of Saturninus: Eclipse of Marius. It is difficult to discern the real Saturninus through the hostile sources. That he genuinely deplored optimate infringement on the powers of the people may well be true. However, in his two tribuneships (103 and 100 B.C.) he did give Marius' veterans more land than they could themselves farm (about 60 acres each). He did conspire to railroad Metellus Numidicus into undeserved exile. He drained the treasury by selling grain to the Roman poor at nominal prices. He supported a false son of Tiberius Gracchus for political purposes. He passed and used as a political tool a treason law (*minuta maiestas*) which was bad because it was vague. Moreover, our informants say, he and his colleagues (especially C. Servilius Glaucia, praetor, 100 B.C.) did not hesitate to use violence in the assemblies.

The political assassination in 100 B.C. of a rival of Glaucia for the consulship led to the demise of this pair. The Senate insisted that the consul, Marius, should act against the lawless violence and passed the Final

Decree. Marius acquiesced so far as to take Glaucia and Saturninus into custody. For temporary safekeeping he put them into the Senate house. A mob, possibly led by retainers of the *optimates*, climbed up on the roof, threw roof tiles down through the rafters, and killed the prisoners. Marius now found himself odious to both factions. He retired from politics and made a tour of the East. He wanted, perhaps, to reconnoiter the ground in Asia Minor where a new war was brewing with Mithradates, King of Pontus.

The Younger Drusus and the Italian Question. In 91 B.C. several important questions of the day came to a focus in the person and program of the younger M. Livius Drusus, son of the opponent of Gaius Gracchus. One of Drusus' chief aims was to obtain citizenship for Italians. Why did the Italians want citizenship? (*See Reading No. 5.*) They were probably not much concerned with the right to vote at Rome. They wanted, simply, to be recognized as equals. They served in the armies which won for Rome both provinces and tribute—but they did not participate equally in the benefits. The lowest-class Romans got subsidized grain. The man who could say "Romanus sum" had advantages over Italian traders. Arbitrary acts of Roman officials in Italy symbolized for Italians their inferior position even if (as seems true) they were not seriously mistreated.

Drusus also wished to shore up senatorial government. He would have enlarged the Senate to include some equestrians. He wanted the Senate to man the permanent extortion court. Equestrian jurors had recently condemned his uncle, P. Rutilius Rufus, whose chief fault was that as a legate in Asia he tried to curb the agents of powerful Roman equestrians. In order to make this extensive program palatable, Drusus, as tribune of the plebs in 91 B.C., passed laws in the Gracchan tradition providing for cheap grain and free land. Supported at first by a powerful coalition of the nobles, he was later suspected of coveting power. Many of the senators turned against him, and he was finally assassinated. At this point the Italians, in despair of justice, took up arms.

The Italian War. This conflict is sometimes called the "Social" war (*socii* = allies). The Italians combined into a well-organized confederacy called "Italia" which must have been long planned. At first they won victories against the ill-prepared Romans. Belatedly the Romans offered citizenship to Italians who did not join the revolt (*Lex Iulia,* 90 B.C.), then to those who would put down their arms (*Lex Plautia-Papiria,* 89 B.C.). This kept the revolt from spreading. Led by men like Marius, Sulla, and the father of Pompey, Roman troops finally crushed those who fought to the bitter end—mostly Samnites. Ultimately, Rome gave the citizenship even to these.

The *optimates* tried to keep the new citizens from voting on an equal basis with other citizens. The *populares* supported the new voters. However, the new ballots seem to have mattered little. There was no new impulse toward democracy. If anything the new voters, especially those in the armies, were even more than the old willing to follow the popular general.

The Mithradatic Wars. Mithradates VI Eupator, king of Pontus (120-63 B.C.) in northern Asia Minor, had long resented the extension of Roman power and influence in Asia, especially in nearby Bithynia. There King Nicomedes II, a client-ally of Rome, blocked Mithradates' aspirations. He persuaded the Romans to force Mithradates out of Cappadocia. The king had occupied this territory while the Romans were fighting the Cimbri and Teutoni. When, therefore, Italy was embroiled in civil war, Mithradates attacked Bithynia, threw out the son of Nicomedes (Nicomedes III), and invaded Roman Asia. Undermanned Roman garrisons could not stop him. Natives everywhere hailed him as a liberator. (*See Reading No. 14C.*) Even the Greeks began to see in him a counterfoil to Roman domination, and Athens made an alliance with him. (*See Reading No. 14D.*) Mithradates now controlled all of Asia Minor and parts of Greece, as well as the rich wheat-producing areas along the north shore of the Black Sea. The king of Armenia was his son-in-law and ally. The monarch was a merciless foe. He decreed death for all Roman citizens in Asia, and it was said that 80,000 were slaughtered in a day.

Struggle in Rome for the Command in the East. The army needed against Mithradates would be large, and it would mean political power for a successful general. The *optimates* picked a political conservative, L. Cornelius Sulla. He was competent and experienced. As

governor of Cilicia a few years before he had successfully
thwarted Mithradates and his son-in-law Tigranes. Since
he was consul in this year (88 B.C.) he was a natural
choice. The Senate allotted to him for the war six legions
which had just been serving under him in the Italian war.

The *populares* also had a logical candidate for the
post. Marius was even more experienced and had had
dealings with Mithradates. A tribune, Sulpicius Rufus,
convened a public assembly and by law appointed Marius
to the command Sulla had been given by decree of the
Senate. Technically, the assembly had this right. A
decision of the people was the highest law. But ever since
the Gracchi and on occasion even before, tribunes had
been using the popular assemblies in ways which in terms
of long-established usage were revolutionary. (*See Reading No. 9F.*) To Sulla the move was an outrageous act
of pure demagoguery. Violence followed. His own son-
in-law was killed, and he himself expelled from Rome.

He fled to his troops. They were willing to follow him
wherever he wished. For the first time then a Roman army
marched on Rome. After a short, sharp fight Sulla occupied the city. Several men were outlawed, including
Rufus (who was soon killed), Gaius Marius, and his
adoptive son of the same name. Marius barely escaped
with his life and took refuge in Africa. Sulla made hasty
dispositions and sailed east (87 B.C.).

The Mithradatic War. Mithradates had made Athens
and its fortified port, the Peiraeus, a base of operations
in Greece. Sulla's first major task was to reduce this base
by siege. By the following year much of the populace
was starving. Athens fell, and after a Pontic withdrawal
by sea, Peiraeus also. The Greeks suffered both in the
siege and at the not-very-tender mercies of Sulla. Two
relieving armies sent by Mithradates via Thrace and
Macedonia came too late. Indeed, Sulla was able to defeat them in detail in two brilliant battles, Chaeronea and
Orchomenus (86 B.C.). He wintered in Greece and collected naval forces to control the Aegean.

In the next year another Roman army led by the
popularis consul for 86 B.C., L. Valerius Flaccus, arrived.
Flaccus was to take over Sulla's command. Sulla refused
to yield, and Flaccus' soldiers refused to fight fellow
Romans. The two armies therefore cooperated in a loose,

haphazard way in the rest of the war. Flaccus was killed by his legate, C. Flavius Fimbria, who took over the army and led it into Asia Minor. He defeated Mithradates and very nearly captured the king. Meanwhile, Sulla too crossed into Asia and found Mithradates ready to accept terms. Because of the threat of Fimbria's army and of a *popularis* overthrow of *optimates* at home, Sulla let the king off lightly. Territorially, he granted Mithradates the *status quo ante bellum*. Mithradates gave up most of his fleet and agreed to pay an indemnity. When Sulla approached Fimbria and his army, most of the troops came over to him, and Fimbria committed suicide.

The Asians who had welcomed Mithradates now had to pay all arrears of taxes at once (five years') and an additional large sum. Some of the cities had been sacked during the conflict. Sulla departed for Rome, leaving L. Licinius Murena, a legate, with an army. Murena soon provoked a sharp battle within the borders of Pontus—and received a setback from Mithradates and a reprimand from Sulla. This indecisive flareup is sometimes called the Second Mithradatic War.

Renewed Civil Conflict. Before leaving for the war with Mithradates, Sulla had executed some *popularis* leaders and exiled others. He had seen that "safe" consuls were elected and had made some changes in the government. All must have seemed secure. However, new conflict soon broke out. Peaceful alternation of parties as in modern two-party democracies was impossible. In familiar pattern, violence and bloodshed gave way to greater violence and bloodshed. The trouble began over the question of equal treatment in the voting tribes for newly enfranchised Italians. The consul, L. Cornelius Cinna, threw in his lot with the *populares*. Marius was recalled from exile, an army was raised, and Rome was again taken by military force. During the years of Sulla's absence the *populares* dominated the city.

Some *optimates* were killed in the fighting; many others were executed without formality. Marius got his seventh consulship (86 B.C.), but died early in the year. Flaccus replaced him. In following years Cinna and the others raised troops to use against Sulla in the East or on his return. Cinna (who served four consecutive years as consul) was killed in 84 B.C. by mutinous soldiers. When Sulla returned to Italy in 83 B.C. his chief opponents were Cn. Papirius Carbo (consul with Cinna in 85 and 84), Marius' son, and the two consuls for 83, L. Cornelius Scipio and C. Norbanus.

Optimate Victories. Scipio's army melted away and mostly went over to Sulla. Young Marius was besieged in Praeneste and finally killed. Carbo, defeated in Etruria, fled, but was finally captured and killed. The bitterest fighting of the civil war erupted at Rome itself in 82 B.C. in the battle of the Colline gate. Samnites formed the core of the opposition. It was said that Sulla butchered 6,000 of them when they surrendered. (*See Reading No. 16A.*) Mopping-up operations were conducted in Sicily, Africa, and Spain. The terror did not end with the fighting. Sulla now proscribed thousands—that is, posted names of persons marked for arbitrary execution. Their property was confiscated and sold. Some of the proceeds went to the depleted coffers of the state. Much found its way into the hands of unscrupulous Sullan supporters. (*See Reading No. 16B.*)

Sulla's Constitutional Measures. Sulla persuaded the subservient remnant of the Senate to declare him Dictator for the Reconstituting of the Republic, a post he held for three years, 82-79 B.C. He revised the constitution, slashing the power of the tribunes and putting the senatorial nobility in firm control of the state. He was not entirely reactionary. Measures enlarging the Senate through automatic admission of quaestors (the number of which was increased to twenty) certainly meant that equestrians and former Latins and Italians might achieve membership. A large number of senators was appointed, not merely to replace those killed in wars and proscriptions, but also to fill the jury-panels. These were now to be made up once more of senators. A renewed *lex annalis* regulated the *cursus honorum*. (*See p. 26.*)

The power of the Senate was restored to what it had been before the Hortensian law of 287 B.C. The powers of the tribal assembly were correspondingly reduced: it could pass laws only with the consent of the Senate. This restriction on the assembly was of course a blow at the tribunes, who now could have little to do with legislation. They were still supposed to protect the plebeians against arbitrary acts of magistrates. Ex-tribunes were barred from higher office. The tribuneship was to be a kind of political dead-end.

In 79 B.C. Sulla astonished Rome when he resigned his dictatorship and retired to his country villa in Campania. Perhaps he was already feeling the disorder which carried him off only a year later. He was alert until a final stroke, able to write extensive *Memoirs* and, according to reports, live voluptuously.

— 9 —

STRUGGLE FOR EQUILIBRIUM, 78-61 B.C.

Dramatis Personae. The story of the troubled *res publica* in its remaining years can only be told in terms of the personalities who so thoroughly dominated it. (*See Reading No. 9D.*) Several of them first began to play important political roles in the period of Sulla's return and reconstitution of the government. Brief introductions are in order.

M. Licinius Crassus (c. 107-53 B.C.) was of distinguished family. Both his father, who had been consul and censor, and his elder brother had been put to death by Cinna and Marius. Crassus hid in Spain. On Sulla's return he went back to Italy and joined Sulla. At the crucial battle at the Colline gate he commanded the victorious wing. He profited in the sale of property of proscribed persons and eventually became the richest man in Rome. He was called Dives, the rich.

M. Tullius Cicero (106-43 B.C.) of Arpinum was born of a good but undistinguished family. He had a good education and oratorical training. He showed great courage in 80 B.C.—as he was not always to do in later career —when he defended the son of a proscribed man against the accusations of Chrysogonus, freedman of Sulla. Cicero attacked Chrysogonus as a rapacious rascal in the trial, though he was careful to suggest that Sulla was not responsible for his freedman's behavior. (*See Reading No. 16B*.) The accused went free, and Cicero was marked as an orator to watch. Meanwhile, he found it advisable to travel in the East for a time.

C. Julius Caesar (c. 100-44 B.C.) at the return of Sulla had already become something of a *popularis* despite his youth and his patrician birth. His Aunt Julia had married Marius. He himself had married Cornelia, the daughter of Cinna. He displeased Sulla when he rejected a suggestion that he divorce Cornelia, but the Dictator merely deprived him of a priesthood to which he had been nominated. Still he, like Cicero, found it expedient to get out of town. He, too, traveled and studied in the East, and returned only after the death of Sulla.

Gn. Pompeius (106-48 B.C.) was the genuine boy wonder of the period. His father, Gn. Pompeius Strabo (consul 89 B.C., a *novus homo*), after long hesitation had led an army for the *optimates* against Cinna and Marius. He was cordially hated by his soldiers, who reported him "killed by lightning" in 87 B.C. On the return of Sulla young Pompey acted with great vigor but with no authority, no office, and only his own money. Starting with a nucleus of family dependents he ultimately raised three full legions. Sulla gave Pompey important assignments in Italy, Sicily, and Africa. He deferred to the young man in quite uncharacteristic fashion, titling him "Imperator" and "Magnus" (which became his surname). He permitted him to celebrate a triumph though he had never held even the quaestorship. Pompey's military precocity made him a popular hero. Unfortunately, he found unprecedented honor and glory a heady tonic for which he retained a habitual appetite.

Threats to the New Order. Sulla had demonstrated how easily a general might seize power; but he had also attempted to restrict ambitious men, especially through his *lex annalis* which regulated office-holding. The example was more likely to endure than the legal barriers. Sulla was scarcely dead before M. Lepidus, consul in 78 B.C., tried to emulate the example. His efforts to change the laws were stymied. So was his attempt to flout

the law by running for successive consulships. He raised
armed rebellion, but his colleague, Q. Catulus, defeated
his attack on Rome. He fled and soon was dead.

Some of the forces of Lepidus took refuge in Spain.
They joined some still unconquered Marians led by Q.
Sertorius. Sertorius had gained the support of the Iberians
and began to represent a real threat to the regime at
Rome. His army cut up several units sent against him.
Pompey demanded the command against Sertorius. Even
his detractors were willing, hoping to get rid of him. He
was given the title of proconsul, for a commander must
necessarily have *imperium*. In Sertorius Pompey more
than met his match. But after several near-disasters he
outlasted his antagonist. A subordinate, jealous of Sertorius, killed him and took over. Pompey in turn eliminated him (72 B.C.), and the Spanish war ended.

Spartacus. There were other woes. In 73 B.C. Spartacus, a Thracian undergoing severe gladiatorial training,
broke out of his Campanian barracks with about seventy
others. They took refuge on Vesuvius. Local militia sent
out against them lost both their weapons and their lives.
Large numbers of slaves escaped and joined Spartacus.
Soon he reportedly had 70,000 or even 120,000 men in
arms. The terror of such a rebellion in a land teeming
with slaves may well be imagined. Successive victories
increased Spartacus' power. In 72 B.C. a major army led
by both consuls was badly beaten.

Late in 72 B.C. Crassus was appointed to this command
(as praetor, propraetor, or proconsul). Early moves by
a lieutenant met with familiar disaster. Crassus was said
to have disciplined one of his units by decimation (executing every tenth man). After a few months Crassus
bottled up Spartacus' forces in the lower peninsula. The
Thracian arranged an evacuation by sea with pirates who
took his money but then doublecrossed him. Finally,
Crassus defeated Spartacus in two hard-fought battles and
(apparently) killed him. Six thousand captives were crucified all along the road from Capua to Rome. But Crassus had to share the glory with Pompey. The latter
arrived in north Italy just in time to massacre several
thousands of the slaves who had escaped Crassus' net.

The Tribuneship Restored. Despite the proscriptions
there remained leaders who wanted a restoration of the

tribunician power. (*See Reading No. 13C.*) Even those who had supported Sulla found some of his laws inconvenient. Changes were inevitable. In 75 B.C., without strong opposition, the right of tribunes to hold further office was again granted.

It was Sulla's lieutenants, Pompey and Crassus, who most drastically undercut the Sullan arrangement. Both ran for the consulship for 70 B.C. According to Sulla's *lex annalis,* Pompey was ineligible, for he had held neither quaestorship nor praetorship. Crassus too was ineligible if he was praetor in 72, for the legal interval between offices was two years. There was even a threat of civil war. Both Pompey and Crassus kept their armies in being. Crassus' decision to join Pompey (there was no love lost between the two) cut short any optimate hopes. To gain popular support the candidates agreed to restore the tribunician powers. In 70 B.C., therefore, tribunes regained all the powers which Sulla had lopped off. The jury system was again overhauled. Equestrians now shared in the jury panels.

Public opinion against the senatorial juries had been stirred up by Cicero. He prosecuted a former governor of Sicily, C. Verres (*see Reading No. 12C, D*) with brilliant and devastating brevity. (Like some of his other extant published speeches the Verrine orations were not delivered in their present form.) In the process he attacked the Sullan jury system, and also showed how rotten some of the ruling class had become.

New Horizons for Pompey. As consul Pompey was ill at ease. He had never sat in the Senate at all, and he had to ask some parliamentarian how to preside at its meetings! The next year neither he nor Crassus held important commands. Crassus' financial operations doubtless kept him busy. Pompey twiddled his thumbs. He could hardly retire at age 37. But only a very important command with very great power could be suitable for such a very great man. (*See Reading No. 15D.*) He had to wait a bit.

The pirates everywhere in the Mediterranean had become quite an irritant. They had made grain prices abnormally high. They had nearly rescued Spartacus. And they were bothersome in other ways. This cause was magnified to a point where it was suitable for Magnus.

A law passed through the assembly by the tribune A. Gabinius in 67 B.C. gave Pompey a huge fleet, a huge army, and almost unlimited funds for a campaign to clear the predators off the sea. The law created a sort of super-command over the littoral of the whole Mediterranean. (*See Reading No. 9E.*) Grain prices immediately plummeted in Rome as speculators unloaded.

Pompey organized his forces admirably. In forty days of operations he cleared the western Mediterranean and in another fifty the whole sea. He raided the pirate strongholds on land, mostly in Cilicia. In humane fashion he settled most of the pirates on vacant lands, where they seem to have done well. It had all been very quick. Mopping-up operations could be conducted by underlings. There was another task which demanded the talents of a Pompey. A third war against Mithradates, King of Pontus, had dragged on for some years in Asia Minor. In 66 B.C. another tribune, C. Manilius, pushed through the assembly a law giving Pompey this added command.

Third Mithradatic War, 74-63 B.C. Relations between Rome and Mithradates had remained basically hostile. The spark which ignited this final conflict was the news, at the death of Nicomedes III of Bithynia, that like Attalus of Pergamum he had willed his kingdom to Rome. Mithradates did not want Roman power at his doorstep. He made alliance with Sertorius (*see p. 69*): he would furnish Sertorius money, Sertorius would send him experienced commanders.

At Rome the war was assigned to L. Licinius Lucullus, consul in 75 B.C. and a firm optimate. He had formerly served against Mithradates as Sulla's naval commander. Lucullus drove Mithradates out of his kingdom and won spectacular victories against Tigranes, King of Armenia, Mithradates' son-in-law and ally. But Lucullus' soldiers, now tired and being asked to serve beyond the legal limit, mutinied. As a result, by 67 B.C. Mithradates was back in Pontus, and the war seemed far from over. Lucullus also had made enemies among Roman equestrians. He had cracked down on their agents who were keeping Asia financially depressed by their exactions. These powerful enemies supported the *Lex Manilia,* mentioned above. When Pompey arrived, Lucullus returned to a grand triumph for his earlier victories and then virtually retired from the public arena to become noted for gross luxury.

Victory and Reorganization of the East. Pompey shortly defeated Mithradates, who was abandoned by Tigranes. The Pontic fox himself escaped to his dominions across the Black Sea and planned a descent on Rome. Pompey, unworried, occupied himself with reorganization. Word soon came that Mithradates was dead, a suicide after a rebellion led by his own son, Pharnaces.

Pharnaces was allowed to keep the European holdings which with Tigranes' Armenia and other kingdoms of Asia Minor became dependent states, allied with Rome. Pontus itself, joined to Bithynia, became a Roman province. Pompey enlarged Cilicia (which had been a province for forty years). He changed all the arrangements of Lucullus. He loaned money to some of the dependent kings which (as we learn from Cicero) they were still trying to pay back years later.

Pompey also moved to the south—no doubt exceeding his authority—and took over Syria, which was in a chaotic state. He intervened in an internal quarrel in Judea and made it also dependent upon Rome. The governor of Syria was expected to keep tab on the little state. His settlement resulted in the rise to power of Antipater and eventually of his son, Herod the Great. Rome now controlled Asia Minor and all the eastern coasts of the Mediterranean to the borders of Egypt.

Cicero's Annus Mirabilis. Cicero's well earned reputation carried him through the *cursus honorum* to the consulship in 63 B.C. at the minimum age. The consulship might have proved difficult except that powerful optimates wished to block the election of L. Sergius Catilinus. Catiline was of patrician family. Dissolute and deeply in debt, he was embittered by this failure to gain election (his second effort). He began to take the popular line and talked loosely of cancelling debts and distributing land.

Next year, when consul, Cicero got wind of a conspiracy instigated by Catiline. Rome was to be set afire, the consuls killed, the state seized. Prompt exposure caused Catiline to flee to the country where he raised an army. In the city several conspirators were picked up and on advice of the Senate executed without trial under authority of the Final Decree. Catiline's army was destroyed. Cicero was titled Father of his Country and ever after sang his own praises in the affair. He had become quite the optimate.

Waiting for Pompey. *Optimates* and even some *populares* dreaded Pompey's return. What would he want next? Would he use his army as a club? There were schemes to gain commands to offset that of Pompey, including a fantastic land bill which Cicero scotched. Some politicians like Caesar sponsored bills to curry favor with Pompey. As for Cicero, he thought the two of them might get on well. He had saved the state at home while Pompey was doing it in the East. Cicero advocated a cooperation of all good men (especially aristocrats and equestrians) in the interest of stability. *Concordia ordinum,* the concord of the orders, he called his scheme. In his view it was a continuation of the best policies of earlier Rome. (*See Reading No. 17.*)

Pompey astounded his suspicious detractors by disbanding his army when he landed in Italy late in 62 B.C. The following year he celebrated a tremendous triumph. He had more than doubled the ordinary revenues of the state. Apparently, he wanted now only to be lionized in grand semi-retirement. He and other Roman politicians were about to learn—unfortunately—that with armies they could be influential, but without troops, frustrated nobodies.

— 10 —

TRIUMVIRATE TO DICTATORSHIP, 60-44 B.C.

The "Three-Headed Monster." Pompey naïvely supposed that no one at Rome would think of denying reasonable requests to one of his great reputation. He wanted only that his numerous acts of reorganization in the East should be registered by the Senate, and that some land be found for his veterans. Routine requests! But he had offended *optimates* when he replaced Lucullus. Also he had not bothered with the usual procedure of conferring with a commission of ten from the Senate when organizing the new provinces.

Outstanding in opposition to Pompey was a great-grandson of Cato the Censor, M. Cato (eventually Uticensis). Cato, a Stoic, posed in the image of his great ancestor. Unfortunately, that put him a century behind the times. He tried to be righteous, but he was also inflexible in minor matters, as no real statesman is. Cato, in his thirties, had held only the office of tribune (62 B.C.). Still, he was already the recognized leader of the more conservative *optimates*.

Cicero too found his influence almost nil despite his tested oratorical ability. He looked on with dismay as the conservatives refused Pompey's requests and alienated him. In the same year powerful equestrians were similarly repelled in the Senate. The *publicani* wanted relief from a contract on which they were suffering large losses. (*See Reading No. 17A.*) Cicero's concordia required the cooperation of nobles and equestrians, and he therefore supported the publicans. But the concordia was not to be.

In this year (60 B.C.) Caesar returned from Spain and appraised the situation. His career had been proceeding well. He was an effective orator in the courts. As aedile in 65 B.C. he treated the crowd at Rome to tremendous games—and he restored Marius' trophies. In 63 B.C. he spent huge sums to gain the office of *pontifex maximus*. The election was important because it symbolized the junking of another of Sulla's laws. After his praetorship (62 B.C.) he was appointed governor of Farther Spain. But so great were his debts that as he was about to leave Italy his baggage was attached! Crassus came to his aid with a large loan.

Caesar now wanted the consulship. A frustrated Pompey and his creditor, Crassus, would help him along. Crassus also had an interest in renegotiating the tax contracts. Pompey still wanted his acts ratified, and he wanted land for his veterans. With skill and tact Caesar persuaded Pompey and Crassus that they should pool their interests. He also made overtures to Cicero, who would make a useful spokesman and mouthpiece. The orator refused. He would have made an awkward member of the team, for he had a few scruples. The expression "three-headed monster" was invented by his friend Varro to describe Caesar's consulship. The term triumvirate is useful, but of course not official.

Caesar's Arrangements. As consul in 59 B.C. Caesar managed affairs for all three. He tried to function within the Senate as a consul normally would. He was blocked there by Cato even when he presented a land bill that was reasonable and should have been passed. He turned to the assembly. Efforts to stop him there brought retaliation; his colleague and opponent M. Bibulus and three tribunes were beaten and driven away. Caesar's bill became law illegally, over the tribunician veto. Other bills reduced the tax contracts and confirmed the acts of Pompey in the East.

Bibulus, afraid for his life, retired to his house and announced from time to time that he was reading the skies. Technically, this meant that the omens were unfavorable and it negated any action of the assembly— or so the *optimates* argued. (*See Reading No. 8.*) One profitable measure of Caesar confirmed Ptolemy Auletes as king of Egypt—for a price. A useful *lex de repetundis* set up a better system for control of extortion in the provinces. The Senate refused to give Caesar a decent command, but a tribune-sponsored bill (*Lex Vatinia*) gave him the provinces of Illyria and Cisalpine Gaul for an unprecedented term of five years. Later the Senate for some reason added to this Transalpine Gaul.

The *optimates* made it clear they would make trouble for the triumvirs the following year. They might even try to annul the legislation *en masse*. Both Cato and Cicero in effect served notice that they did not intend to acquiesce in the new order. Caesar therefore tried to elect new officials who would look out after his interests in his absence.

P. Clodius Pulcher, Tribune of the Plebs, 58 B.C. Clodius (his way of spelling Claudius) was a patrician. But Caesar arranged his adoption into a plebeian family to make him eligible for the tribuneship. Clodius in 62

B.C. had been caught in Caesar's house during rites to the Bona Dea which were for women only. He was at least trying to have an affair with Caesar's wife. Caesar then divorced his wife but refused to testify against Clodius when he was prosecuted. (*See Reading No. 17A.*) Perhaps this is the manner in which he got Clodius in his pocket. Caesar had divorced his wife only because she must be above suspicion, he said. His own sexual morals were notoriously bad. It was a good joke.

Clodius hated Cicero, who had testified against him in the trial and who had twitted him unmercifully with his caustic tongue. Now Clodius got revenge and popularity at the same time. Cicero was vulnerable. As consul he had put Roman citizens to death without trial, much less appeal. He had acted under the Final Decree and advice of the Senate, but this the *populares* never admitted to be constitutional. Clodius got a bill passed exiling the orator, who spent a miserable year and a half in Macedonia and Greece. Meanwhile Clodius tore down three of his houses. His mansion on the Palatine was replaced by a shrine to Liberty.

It was difficult to recall Cicero, even after Clodius' tribuneship expired. Clodius—and all other important men at Rome—had numerous adherents. Clodius had formed his men into the roughest gang in town. (*See Reading No. 18.*) Not until the optimate T. Milo organized a rival gang as tough could anything be done. Cicero returned to a grand reception by the fickle mob, but he was a chastened man. For some years he pretty well toed the triumvirs' line. He did get his property back, with compensation.

Cato was got rid of more simply. He was made propraetor and sent to organize a new province, Cyprus— to which the Romans had no real claim. Cato was not bothered by the ethics of the situation. His treatment of the scion of the Ptolemaic line who claimed to be king of Cyprus soon drove the latter to suicide. On the island young Marcus Brutus, nephew to Cato, made some very shady fiscal arrangements of which Cato can hardly have been unaware. Special senatorial decrees were passed to make Brutus' deal possible. (*See Reading No. 9C.*) Cato's shining sword had a ragged edge.

Renewal of the Triumvirate, 56 B.C. There was always danger that the informal triumvirate might fall apart. Pompey and Crassus disliked each other. Clodius irritated Pompey. (*See Reading No. 18.*) Caesar seemed to be getting the best of the bargain. And optimate leaders, especially those connected closely with Cato, tried to split the three. The year 56 B.C. was critical for Caesar. His command was running out. *Optimates* intended to prosecute him when he no longer had magisterial immunity. One of the candidates for the consulship for 55 B.C. was a particular enemy.

To repair fences Caesar called a grand conference at Luca in Cisalpine Gaul. Besides Pompey and Crassus numerous other officials and senators attended. It was agreed that Pompey and Crassus should have the consulship for the following year, and then extraordinary commands. They would thus gain a kind of equality with Caesar, who stipulated only an extension of his present command. A little more than usual of violence and bribery were required in the elections, but the returns were right. Pompey chose a five-year command in Spain, Crassus in Syria, where it would be easy to stir up a war with the Parthians.

Crassus Killed at Carrhae, 53 B.C. Crassus aspired to a military reputation to match those of his partners. His preparations in Syria for invasion of Parthia included seizure of the temple treasuries at Hierapolis and Jerusalem. In summer of 53 B.C. he moved his army across the Euphrates and into the desert. But this terrain suited the kind of warfare the Parthians knew best. Crassus' army was riddled by mounted archers. The Roman cavalry under Publius, son of Crassus, was lured into a fatal trap. The main army now fell back. At Carrhae, most of the army and Crassus himself were annihilated. According to one story the Parthians used the head of Crassus in a realistic performance of Euripides' *Bacchae*. A few Roman soldiers under C. Cassius, a quaestor, escaped. Cassius competently organized the defense of Syria and saved the province from retaliatory invasion by the Parthians.

Caesar in Gaul. The "Gauls" who inhabited the area of present-day France were mostly semi-civilized Celts. When Caesar became governor of Transalpine Gaul

a migrating Celtic tribe, the Helvetii, were threatening
to invade Gaul. Behind and to the north of them German
tribes were similarly on the move. Caesar thwarted the
Helvetians and campaigned to the Rhine against the expanding Suebi. Thereafter, he apparently decided on
conquest of the whole territory.

The nine-year campaign of conquest Caesar led with
efficiency and the best kind of publicity through the lucid,
straightforward prose of his *Gallic Wars*. He made two
thrusts into England, but with no lasting effect. Campaigns into Germany itself put down the threat of invasion there. His bridge across the Rhine astonished and
impressed the Germans. One need only remember how
recently the Cimbri and Teutoni had swept all before
them—until Marius stopped them—to understand the
immense popularity Caesar gained through these operations. Although Caesar on occasion brutally massacred
men, women, and children, this was not his usual practice. His settlement in Gaul was sound and lasting.

Rebellions in Gaul in the winter of 54 B.C.—and even
more dangerously, under Vercingetorix in 52 B.C.—put
the Romans to a severe test. Pompey even lent a legion
to Caesar (who now had twelve). After the crisis, in
50 B.C., the Senate asked from Caesar and Pompey a
legion each to protect the eastern frontiers. Caesar was
in turn asked by Pompey to return the borrowed one.
Consequently, Caesar had to send two of his legions to
Italy. He sent them with warm compliments and high
bonuses.

Pompey's Rule in Rome. Pompey, as proconsul of
Spain and also prefect of the Roman grain supply, had
a choice of location. He stayed in Rome and ruled Spain
through legates. In the city, violence mounted, especially
at the elections. The chief instigators were the rival gangs
of Clodius and Milo. Elections at times were postponed
for months. Early in 52 B.C. at a chance encounter near
Rome, Milo killed Clodius. The latter's followers burnt
his body publicly—along with the senate-house and other
buildings. The city was in anarchy.

Pompey was now made sole consul (an alternative to
dictatorship) and restored order. Cicero's somewhat
timorous defense was not enough to keep Milo from a
court conviction and exile. A law of Pompey set a five-
year interval between the holding of office and the gov-

erning of a province. This created a shortage of governors. Cicero (who was eligible) agreed to govern Cilicia. Another law required candidates for office to appear personally in Rome. And another extended Pompey's own command in Spain for five years. Each of these laws was at least potentially adverse to Caesar.

Caesar and Pompey Come to a Rupture. The death of Crassus strained relations between Caesar and Pompey. The death in childbirth (54 B.C.) of Julia, daughter of Caesar and wife of Pompey, destroyed a link which had bound them together. The continued successes of Caesar aroused Pompey's ego. He could brook no equal in reputation. The efforts of the *optimates* to win over Pompey began at last to bear fruit.

By 50 B.C. the rift between the two widened and approached a crisis. Considering the times, Caesar's demands were not exorbitant. He wanted to run for a second consulship without giving up command of his army. Caesar soon even offered to give up both his province and his army if Pompey would do the same. Bolstered by extreme conservative support, Pompey refused. He apparently felt Caesar should be cut down to size. In January, 49 B.C., the Senate voted to replace Caesar and expelled tribunes (like M. Antony) who tried to protect his interests. The Final Decree was passed.

Caesar, then, had to make a decision. He could see his career ruined or plunge the state into civil war. Faced with a choice like that he never hesitated. He crossed the Rubicon, and the war was on.

The Civil War: Rubicon to Ilerda. When Caesar invaded Italy he had less than a full legion at hand. The rest of his men were in Gaul. But Pompey was depending on new levies and on the two legions which Caesar had recently sent to Italy. Caesar swiftly gained towns and troops, and ultimately the two key legions came over to him also. Still other troops began to arrive from Gaul. Pompey, who had once remarked that he had merely to stamp his feet and troops would spring forth from the ground (*see Reading No. 15D*), found it was not so simple. He and his supporters abandoned Rome. In their haste they left the treasury behind; Caesar found it quite useful. Caesar tried to cut off Pompey in South Italy, but Pompey moved across to Epirus without loss. All of Italy was Caesar's.

Caesar marched to Rome, interviewing along the way Cicero, recently back from Cilicia. Cicero was still hoping to mediate between the two titans. He found neither side palatable. Eventually he joined Pompey, but quite without enthusiasm. In Rome Caesar got a rather cold reception. He warmed up the rabble with gifts of money and grain, but repelled them when he threatened a tribune in order to get at the public money. The rump of the Senate granted some of his dispositions, but rejected others.

Before Caesar could pursue Pompey he must remove a threat from Spain and Massilia in south France. Moving quickly as always, Caesar soon had Massilia under siege. Then he crossed into Spain. He was slowed by rains and high water, but at Ilerda he outmaneuvered and reduced his opponents. In little more than a month all of Pompey's forces in Spain were defeated or had surrendered. Caesar was lenient—as he had been in the entire campaign—and permitted whoever would to leave and join Pompey. Most of the troops, however, enlisted under his banner. He now moved north again, to preside over the surrender of Massilia.

Back in Rome news of the victories produced a change of heart. The Senate named Caesar dictator—a post which allowed him to preside over elections. Once he arrived this was one of the chief items of business. Somehow he was himself elected to the consulship. He carried some measures for the relief of debtors and a few other items of civil procedure. His primary concern was the conduct of the war.

Victory at Pharsalus. Pompey controlled the sea. This should have been a decisive factor in the war, but Caesar managed to get his legions safely across the Adriatic. Even then, Caesar was outnumbered and indeed suffered reverses when he attempted to besiege Pompey's forces at Dyrrhachium. Caesar's move to Thessaly was primarily dictated by a need for supplies. There Pompey's superior cavalry should have meant a great advantage. The decision of Pompey to engage in full force (Pharsalia, August, 48 B.C.) was a mistake, even though Caesar was heavily outnumbered. Many of Pompey's men were new levies, and they simply could not stand up to veterans. Caesar's clever use of reserves at a decisive point broke Pompey's army.

Interlude in Egypt. Pompey fled. Caesar followed. News of Pharsalia preceded Pompey, and the erstwhile conqueror of the East could find no welcome anywhere. He ruled against a long journey to Africa where he had some troops. In Egypt the son and daughter of Ptolemy Auletes might remember with gratitude his role in restoring their father to power. But young Ptolemy's advisers decided Pompey's presence would be embarrassing; he was deceived and assassinated before he reached shore.

Caesar arrived in Alexandria shortly. It was said he wept when told of Pompey and refused to look at the head, which had been saved for him. He probably tried to collect money still owing for the restoration of Ptolemy Auletes. Natives were soon declaring that he acted less like a foreign visitor than a conquering general. The twenty-one-year-old Cleopatra persuaded him to champion her claims against her brother (they were already at war over who should have the sole rule). The reaction brought Caesar and his small contingent of troops into the war, and he was soon besieged in Alexandria. He sent for help and took energetic measures to defend his position. Eventually succor came. He left Egypt at last, leaving Cleopatra queen—and pregnant. She soon had a child, which she named Caesarion. Caesar never acknowledged the child, but he did not object to the name and later entertained Cleopatra at his house in Rome.

One further task required his attention in the East. Pharnaces, son of Mithradates, had taken advantage of the confusion of the civil war and the Egyptian affair to defy a lieutenant of Caesar's and seized territories both Roman and allied. Caesar's campaign was nearly as short as his famous message to Rome following: *veni, vidi, vici*. Caesar had now been absent from Rome for well over a year. In his absence his opponents had taken new hope and his followers were quarreling. It was high time the master returned to set things right.

The African Campaign. In Rome Caesar compromised between his feuding followers. He gave the populace of Rome free rent for a year and cut interest on debts, but he refused to cancel all debts as some of his radical followers proposed. The propertied classes were generally reassured by him. His clemency toward persons like Cicero won over some former opponents. Antony, who had been left in charge in Rome, lost favor because of the crude and brutal way he had handled popular agitation aroused by radicals like Dolabella. When a mutiny of veteran troops broke out in Campania, Sallust, the later historian, could not quell it and nearly lost his life trying. Caesar put it down in minutes. In general his formula for handling troops was to make them extravagant promises in crises and then to live up to the promises (for survivors) no matter how much property had to be confiscated to do it.

Under the leadership of Cato and Q. Metellus Scipio (consul 52 B.C.) *optimates* had gathered new forces in north Africa for a stand against Caesar. Again the decision must depend on battle. Caesar required some months to establish a beachhead in Africa and to collect and train the necessary forces. When he was ready he cleverly forced Scipio's army to move out of its strongly held fortifications by threatening the town of Thapsus. The battle near there in April, 46 B.C., was a rout. Scipio committed suicide when about to be captured. Cato, who had been left in charge at Utica, likewise did away with himself. The event was later sentimentalized by nostalgic *optimates,* and Cato was posthumously awarded the surname Uticensis.

Back in Rome Caesar celebrated four tremendous triumphs. It would have been unseemly to triumph over Romans; his were over the Gauls, the Egyptians, the Pontians (Pharnaces), and the Africans (King Juba). Besides the usual bloody games he also staged a realistic naval battle in an artificial lake. Vercingetorix made his funeral march in the first triumph, and the younger sister of Cleopatra adorned the second. For Romans it was quite a holiday.

Second Spanish Campaign. Thapsus should have ended the civil war. But under the leadership of Labienus, a former lieutenant of Caesar in Gaul and now one of his most implacable enemies, and two sons of Pompey the Great, Gnaeus and Sextus, a new threat built up in Spain. Refugees from the African debacle fled to Spain. They were joined by some Caesarian legions and Spanish natives. The disaffection was primarily the result of rivalry and maladministration on the part of Caesar's commanders in the peninsula.

The final, decisive struggle at Munda came in the

Spring of 45 B.C. The battle was hard-fought and bloody. Caesar had generally spared the conquered. However, many of the enemy had enjoyed Caesar's clemency once. They were not to be forgiven a second time. Moreover, his soldiers were disgruntled at the unwarranted continuation of the war. Thousands of troops were slaughtered and the nearest town of any size, Corduba, was sacked. Labienus and Gnaeus Pompey died. Only Sextus Pompey escaped, salvaging naval contingents which were to trouble the successors of Caesar. On his return Caesar celebrated a fifth great triumph—over the Spaniards, of course.

Caesar's Civil Administration. Scholars have argued bitterly over Caesar's permanent accomplishments. He was not in power long enough, actually, for any real assessment to be made. About some of his arrangements we are ill informed; we know something of his plans for the future, but plans are not easily translated into deeds. Surely he would have run the empire more efficiently and with more regard for the provincials than the oligarchy had.

Caesar brought some provincials into the government with full citizenship; he even introduced Gauls into the Senate (which he enlarged to about 900). He limited terms of governors and revised the publican tax system in Asia. He reformed the calendar, adopting the solar year. In the process he made 46 B.C. into a very long year of about 435 days. He settled thousands of veterans and poor citizens of Rome on farms in Italy and in the provinces. He was able to reduce by half the number of persons receiving free grain in the city. He added in Rome a new forum, a large basilica, a new temple. Numerous other projects were carried through or planned.

The Ides of March. The moribund "Republic" to which Caesar gave the death blow was really an ingrown and inflexible oligarchy. For decades the oligarchs had given little more than lip service to the customs of the ancestors (*mos maiorum*). Government by constitutional law which was superior to every individual had scarcely existed since the days of the Scipios. Nevertheless, there were those who still took the old ideals seriously. Men like Cicero, for example, even reinforced the old views by associating them with widely accepted Stoic teachings (as in *De Re Publica*). It was, therefore, a serious mistake on Caesar's part to flout the old system as he flaunted his new powers.

Before 49 B.C. Caesar had been perhaps willing to be merely one of two or more persons who dominated the constitution. But now he spoke openly of his *"dominatus,"* and he held offices to match. He was consul most years from 49 B.C. to his death, and in 45 consul without colleague. He held the powers of a tribune and of a censor. After holding the dictatorship for short periods he became dictator for ten years, and early in 44 he assumed the title for life. Some of his coins proclaim the "perpetual dictator." He rigged the elections even years in advance. Prefects appointed by him took over functions of quaestors and praetors. It was widely rumored and believed that he wanted to take the title of king. Probably the famous scene at the Lupercalia when Antony offered the crown to Caesar was deliberately staged so that Caesar could show Romans that the rumor was groundless. He declared that Romans had no king but Jupiter and sent the crown to adorn the god's image. What need had Caesar of another and empty title?

Probably it was Caesar's assumption of the title of perpetual dictator which brought to a head the conspiracy which took his life March 15, 44 B.C. He was stabbed to death at the foot of a statute of Pompey in the Senate house. The chief conspirators were Gaius Trebonius, Gaius Cassius, Decimus and Marcus Brutus (distant cousins). Trebonius and Decimus Brutus had been Caesarian officers for some years. Decimus Brutus was even named as a second-degree heir in Caesar's will. Cassius and Marcus Brutus had fought with Pompey, but had been pardoned by Caesar. For Marcus, Caesar had some affection, possibly because he had had an affair with Brutus' mother, Servilia, some years before. The "Liberators" or "Tyrannicides" (as they called themselves) were sure they had only to kill the "tyrant" to restore "freedom." Several additional years of civil war would show how mistaken they were.

FROM OCTAVIUS TO AUGUSTUS

Confusion Following the Murder of Caesar. The conspirators had made few plans beyond killing the "tyrant." They expected to get broad support in the Senate. One of them had a speech prepared. But the senators, frightened by the uproar, got themselves home behind bars as soon as possible. The conspirators thought that even the mob might praise a new era of freedom. Again, someone was to orate a bit, and they had carefully planted a few persons in the crowd to shout slogans at the right times. But wild rumor and apprehension brought confusion and pell-mell dispersion. The conspirators ran through the city trying to spread good news and assurance. They got an impression of an ugly time to come. They therefore gathered on the Capitoline hill and barricaded themselves in a temple. (*See Reading No. 19.*)

When Antony heard of the murder of Caesar he was sure that he was number two on the list. He fortified himself in his house and awaited the worst. The conspirators had convinced themselves that their motives were idealistic. They had, therefore, decided that they would kill neither Antony, the consul, nor Marcus Lepidus, Master of the Horse. Thus they would prove to the world that there was nothing personal in the assassination: it was a matter of principle. As it happened, Lepidus had a legion of troops just outside the city. Upon receiving news of the assassination he brought his men into Rome and maintained order in support of the Caesarians.

Caesarians and Liberators: A Modus Vivendi. Why were the assassins not eliminated by Antony, Lepidus, and the Caesarian consul-designate P. Dolabella? Their forbearance certainly was not due to sympathy with republican views. Their inaction may be attributed to uncertainty, indecision, and rivalry. Antony did make one significant move: from Calpurnia, Caesar's widow, he obtained Caesar's papers and his money—presumably state funds. The three moved cautiously and came to temporary terms with the conspirators.

When the Senate was called into session, the orator Cicero persuaded all concerned to adopt a conciliatory middle course. By a sort of amnesty the murderers were freed from fear of prosecution. On the other hand all of Caesar's acts and dispositions, even for the future, were confirmed by the Senate. Some reactionaries were willing to risk chaos by nullifying all of Caesar's acts. Cicero hoped that the Caesarians could be eased out of positions of power and the republican forms re-established.

Antony steered an equivocal course. Permitted to give Caesar a public funeral, he stirred the crowd to the point of a major riot. Caesar's body was cremated right there in the forum. A man who was mistakenly identified as one of the Liberators was torn to pieces. However, it was Antony who proposed that the very office of dictator should be abolished—a reflection on the dead dictator, but also reassuring to those *optimates* who saw in him another Caesar. It was, perhaps, inevitable that the Senate and the Caesarians should clash in the old ways, over the same issues. Antony, for example, got the assembly to decree him the province he wanted when the Senate refused to do it. It was the old cycle: the *popularis* leader backed by the assembly defied the Senate over commands, power, armies, and lucrative provinces.

Caesar's Heir: A Third Force. No one took any account of the young man who would one day end the civil conflict and seize personal control of the empire. He was Gaius Octavius, a grand-nephew of Caesar (grandson of Caesar's sister Julia), only eighteen years old. Caesar provided in his will that Octavius should be his adopted son and principal heir. When the adoption was registered, he was known as Gaius Julius Caesar Octavianus, hence modern historians' use of the name Octavian. He is best known to history as Augustus, a name conferred upon him in 27 B.C.

The middle of March found Octavius in Epirus with some of Caesar's legions, which were to be used in a projected campaign against Parthia. He was designated Master of the Horse. He would have taken office when Lepidus resigned to govern Narbonensian Gaul. After a messenger brought the news of Caesar's death, Octavius hesitated only briefly before he headed for Rome. On his way to the city he learned of his adoption. Some of Caesar's veterans hailed him as "Caesar." It was an auspicious beginning.

At Rome Octavian (as we shall now call him though the adoption was not yet legalized) got no welcome from Antony and Dolabella. Antony refused to turn over Caesar's money to the heir on the ground (no doubt) that it really belonged to the state. Octavian sold some inherited property and carried out a popular feature of Caesar's will. The late dictator had bequeathed seventy-five *denarii* to every Roman citizen—presumably those resident in the city. Octavian was soon wooing and winning the allegiance of many of Caesar's veterans. Some of the soldiers, especially the semiprofessional military tribunes, deplored the rift between Antony and Octavian. For the time they could not moderate between the two.

Cicero: A Last Great Effort. The disputes involving provinces and armies, meanwhile, ended the cautious truce between Antony and the senatorial leaders. Cicero was now at the head of those who hoped to restore the oligarchy which they called a republic. The aging orator saw reason for hope in the break between young Octavian and Antony and in the strong positions held by some of the assassins. Decimus Brutus had been given Cisalpine Gaul by Caesar. The province was, of course, in a very strategic location, close to Rome. Trebonius had similarly been given Asia. Marcus Brutus, without authorization, seized Macedonia and Cassius, Syria. The Senate later legalized their positions.

The focus of renewed civil conflict was to be Cisalpine Gaul. Antony got the assembly to give it to him, as has been said. When Decimus Brutus showed defiance, Antony got together an army to force him out. At this point Cicero began to thunder against Antony in a series of speeches and pamphlets which he called Philippics after the orations of Demosthenes against Philip of Macedonia three centuries before. Most were delivered after Antony had already left Rome. Cicero successfully aroused widespread opposition to Antony. Brutus took up a strong position in Mutina. The Senate sent him word to hold out.

Senatorial Victory Turned into Defeat. The consuls for 43 B.C., G. Pansa and A. Hirtius, raised troops for the relief of Mutina. The soldiers of young Octavian were formed into a proper army. Octavian himself was given the power of a praetor (*imperium pro praetore*). He had made fantastic promises to his soldiers, and the Senate now agreed to raise the money to give substance to them. The Senate also got hold of a fleet by legitimizing the command of Sextus Pompey.

A major battle came in April. The senatorial armies drove Antony from the field with heavy losses. This victory, which conceivably might have made possible Cicero's fondest hopes, was turned into defeat because both Hirtius and Pansa were killed. Young Octavian now controlled the bulk of the army. He did not follow up the victory. In August, in fact, he menaced the Senate with his troops and got himself named consul. He had first to look out for himself. He was under no misapprehension. It was common knowledge that Cicero and the Senate intended to make use of this nineteen-year-old boy and then get rid of him.

Antony used the period of grace to merge with Lepidus and the latter's army in Narbonensian Gaul, perhaps against the real wishes of Lepidus. Antony was personally popular with Lepidus' troops. Octavian now faced a much stronger foe. He decided to join them. In November, 43 B.C., therefore, the three got together and formed a second triumvirate. This one was later given official status.

Proscriptions Once Again. The triumvirs used Sullan methods to get rid of prominent opponents. Cicero's name was high on the list. He was soon killed. Antony's wife Fulvia was said to have stuck pins through his tongue as his severed head hung in the Forum. Several hundred other persons made up the list, including, of course, all the assassins of Caesar. Leaders on both sides prepared energetically for a new trial by battle.

One of the chief conspirators was already dead. Trebonius, in Asia, permitted Dolabella to pass through the province. But the latter murdered Trebonius and took over. Shortly thereafter Cassius came up from Syria and avenged Trebonius: Dolabella was a suicide. The next of the conspirators to go was Decimus Brutus. His position was untenable after the merger cut away his support, and he was killed while attempting to flee.

The Battles of Philippi. Marcus Brutus and Gaius Cassius made a strong stand against Antony and Octavian. They taxed the resources of the East and assembled a formidable army. Two battles fought near Philippi in Macedonia in the autumn of 42 B.C. were decisive. The first battle moved in a gigantic cartwheel. The right wing of each army overwhelmed the opposing left. Antony led the successful assault on one side and Marcus Brutus on the other. Cassius, thinking that Brutus also had lost, committed suicide just as some of his officers rode up to tell him of victory on the right. Octavian, perhaps, thought all was lost too, as his camp was plundered. But he was not the type to rush into suicide. Following defeat in the second battle Brutus in turn committed suicide. Serious problems still faced the victors. Octavian went back to meet the difficulties in Italy. He was physically ill, as he had been most of the time during the campaign. Antony went east to take over territories which had been held by the assassins and to deal with the Parthian threat.

Octavian Copes with the West. The tasks which Octavian faced might have seemed insuperable to a less determined young man of 21. He needed money and land for his troops and veterans. Land recently confiscated from proscribed persons had gone to veterans or had been sold for cash. The triumvirs had also resorted to confiscatory taxation of the rich to provide the sinews of war. Now, a few short months later, the need was as great as ever. Troops in these times demanded and got high bonuses. They could be controlled in no other way. Somehow Octavian managed it, but he made many enemies.

The third member of the triumvirate, Lepidus, posed another problem. Apparently, he played an undercover game against Octavian and Antony and negotiated with Sextus Pompey. Or perhaps Octavian and Antony simply decided to freeze him out. The latter two reshuffled provinces, virtually dispossessing Lepidus of command. When he no longer seemed a threat, Octavian permitted him to govern Africa.

Sextus Pompey himself presented a much more serious

threat. He had control of the western seas and had gained Sicily as an island base. He could harass shipping —his opponents thought him no better than a pirate— and he could cut off much of the food supply of Rome any time he chose. He still had support in Italy from such republicans as had managed to survive and from many who wanted the wars to end. For the time Octavian could do nothing about Pompey.

Those who wished to see a genuine effort to restore the republican constitution included, surprisingly, the brother of Antony, Lucius, who was consul in 41 B.C. He championed the ordinary magistracies and opposed further confiscation and distribution of land. He got strong support from Fulvia, the wife of Mark Antony, a woman of remarkably strong will. Her primary motive was to guard her husband's interests, to prevent Octavian from becoming too strong. This rivalry mounted until it broke out into brief armed conflict. The struggle centered at Perusia. Octavian besieged and finally took the town. Lucius he treated gently, but Perusian leaders he executed. The impression of clemency and tolerance associated with the name of Augustus derives mostly from a later era. Fulvia fled. She joined her husband, who berated her for her rash actions. She soon died.

Antony and the East. Antony, meanwhile, consolidated his power in the East. Although Cassius and Brutus had thoroughly fleeced the area of money and supplies, Antony was able to repeat the exorbitant demands. What could the provincials do but pay? In one province they paid nineteen years of normal taxes to the two sides in four years.

Antony's meeting with Cleopatra and their subsequent relations are well known. He commanded her to come to his headquarters and explain her support of the conspirators. According to Plutarch she arrived in an elaborate barge adorned with purple sails and silver oars. When Antony met her on deck she was dressed like Aphrodite and her court maids as nymphs. Antony forgot about reproaches. He had the soldier's tendency to take life easy in winter after a hard summer's campaigning. The winter of 41-40 he spent in Alexandria with the Egyptian (really Greek) queen. He knew nothing of the privations his brother and his wife were suffering at Perusia.

A New Accord. There were tense moments in the following year when Antony returned to Italy. His army and Octavian's squared off militarily near Brundisium. But followers of both pressed for a settlement of differences, and Antony and Octavian agreed to confer. They decided to maintain a general division of Roman dominions, Antony taking the East and Octavian Italy and the West. They patched up things with Lepidus, but he only retained Africa. Some months later the two even confirmed Sextus Pompey's hold over both Sicily and Sardinia. To strengthen the accord Antony married Octavia (Fulvia was now dead), sister of the triumvir.

Antony spent this winter in Greece in the company of his new wife. Meanwhile, affairs in Syria were going well. The Parthians, led by a Roman *optimate*, Labienus, presented a dangerous threat. They were turned back by Ventidius, a competent lieutenant of Antony.

Sextus Pompey and Marcus Lepidus Stripped of Power. The basic antagonism between Octavian and Sextus Pompey prevented any permanent accommodation. Octavian soon got an opportunity to seize Sardinia from Pompey and did. Pompey of course retaliated by cutting the Roman grain supply. It came to war. Octavian's first efforts to defeat Pompey at sea were disastrous. In 36 B.C., however, Octavian's trusted lieutenant Marcus Agrippa crushed Pompey's fleet. The reduction of Sicily followed shortly. Pompey fled east, but was killed by one of Antony's officers.

Marcus Lepidus tried to make capital out of the campaign. He did cooperate with Octavian in Sicily. But when Pompey's infantry surrendered to him rather than to Octavian, the temptation was great. He defied Octavian; apparently he intended to press for an equal role in the unbalanced triumvirate (which had been officially renewed the year before). Octavian acted courageously. He appeared among Lepidus' men and won over most of his opponent's army without a fight. Lepidus was now unofficially deposed. He was kept virtual prisoner in Italy until his death years later. Possibly it was his position as *pontifex maximus* which kept him from execution.

Antony's Parthian Expedition. By 37 B.C. Antony had completed his reorganization of Roman territory in the East. Now he was ready for more exciting things.

These included a war against Parthia and a return to the arms of Cleopatra. Octavia and her small Antonia were soon sent home to Rome. Cleopatra suited Antony's personality better than did Octavia, who seems to have been the meek, domestic type. Antony had become a god of sorts. He liked to appear at feasts and festivals garbed as Dionysus (Latin, Pater Liber) as he had done even at Rome. Cleopatra as Isis (Aphrodite) spiced such celebrations. Eventually, the two were formally married, it seems. It did not matter much to Octavia—or to Octavian—that under Egyptian law such a marriage could have been legal.

The invasion of Parthia got under way in the spring of 36 B.C. To avoid the mistakes of Crassus, Antony moved north from Antioch and east into Armenia, a dependent, allied state. On the trek south into Parthian lands he did not adequately protect his heavy baggage and siege train. Parthian cavalry attacked and destroyed most of it. Antony was now unable to reduce any important fortress. He did not have adequate supplies, and Parthian superiority in cavalry made it difficult to live off the land. Armenia began to withdraw allegiance.

There was nothing to do but to retreat. Here Antony demonstrated his resourcefulness as a commander, but on the march back to Syria wintry weather, inadequate supplies, and harassment from enemy cavalry whittled his once strong army to a pitiful remnant. The expedition had been a great loss, but it was not a disaster. Soon Antony was able to take advantage of a quarrel between Medes and Parthians and to make an alliance with the Medes. He was left free to punish Armenia (35-34 B.C.) and indeed seized the king himself. Back in Alexandria he celebrated a kind of triumph.

A New Struggle for Supreme Power. By 33 B.C. Octavian had secured all the west. He had regained control of areas in Illyria and Dalmatia which had been lost to Rome since the civil wars of Pompey and Caesar. By the same year Antony had somewhat reduced Parthian power; he regained the standards lost in his earlier invasion fiasco. The two dynasts could give more attention to each other. Relationships between them now swiftly deteriorated into war.

There is no point in trying to assess blame. Octavian resented the treatment of his sister, who was at length formally divorced. Naked ambition played its part. Antony might have been satisfied with the eastern half of the empire—plus some territories further east. He and Cleopatra were reported to have half-formed plans to follow in the footsteps of Alexander.

Some of Antony's behavior formed excellent grist for Octavian's propaganda mills. (*See Reading No. 20.*) Antony dallied with Cleopatra while Octavia in Rome faithfully took care of all his children, including Fulvia's. He and Cleopatra appeared as gods in Alexandria in a celebration during which they made the famous "donations of Alexandria"—gifts for their son, Alexander Helios, and for Caesarion, son of Caesar. These gifts included some territories belonging to Rome. Antony presented additional Roman territory (Syria, Cyprus, Libya) to Cleopatra herself. Octavian publicized these scandalously un-Roman actions. He also got hold of Antony's will from the Vestal Virgins and announced that in it Antony requested burial in Alexandria. Most reprehensible for a Roman.

Actium and After. Despite all this adverse publicity Antony still had surprisingly strong support in Italy and Rome. Octavian had shown few of the strong qualities for which he was later praised. He had had to confiscate land and levy high and unpopular taxes. Perhaps some of the feeling for Antony was only feeling against the nearest of the two despots.

Antony, with much help from Cleopatra (too much, many of his staff felt) collected troops and ships at Samos and then crossed over into Greece. He established a strong position at Actium on the Ionian Sea. Apparently he intended to invade Italy itself. It probably could have been done if he had acted in 32 B.C. However, he delayed unaccountably long. Octavian, or perhaps one should say Agrippa, who did most of the work, got a force across the Adriatic and invested Actium by land and sea.

Antony delayed the showdown battle (did he hope even yet for an accommodation?) until large contingents of his troops began to desert. Forced to a decision, he finally got set for a sea battle (Actium, 31 B.C.). Apparently Cleopatra, who commanded a division of her own ships, came out prepared to flee: she carried money and equipment that would not ordinarily have been taken into bat-

tle. The struggle was not yet decided when she fled. When
Antony saw it, we are told, he got into a smaller vessel,
overtook her flagship, and went aboard. Thus, incredibly,
he in effect abandoned both fleet and army. He and Cleopatra went on to Egypt. Antony's men soon surrendered.
They were treated well by Octavian. By the next year
(30 B.C.) he was ready to press into Egypt itself.

In Egypt Antony had dropped into deep depression
and had done almost nothing. Cleopatra still had gran-
diose ideas. She attempted to move her ships over the
desert to the Red Sea (apparently for use in some eastern
campaign), but marauding Arabs burned them. Client
princes in large numbers had defected to Octavian, but
at length a small defense force was assembled. Once
hostile troops arrived there was little fighting. Antony
committed suicide after hearing a false report that
Cleopatra had already done so. A few days later, after
her womanly wiles failed on Octavian, Cleopatra similarly
took her own life. She had said that she would never be
led in triumph through Rome.

Octavian, still only 33 years of age, was at last sole
ruler.

— 12 —

EPILOGUE

There was no more effective opposition to one-man
rule at Rome. One reason is that many of the nobles—
the most likely opponents—were dead. Only the nobles
really equated freedom with the traditional oligarchy.
This "freedom" of course meant privilege and opportunity
to hold high and lucrative positions in government. We
need not think their motives had been only greed. They
were no doubt convinced that they were better qualified
to rule than any other conceivable group, that the "re-

public" afforded the best possible governmental structure. And indeed, Augustus found it necessary to resuscitate—but to broaden—privileged classes very like those he had helped to destroy. To be sure, the new classes must function always under the shadow of the *princeps,* as he liked to be called.

As for the provinces, how could they lose through peace? Especially in the richer areas of the east, provincials had been mulcted of income and capital again and again in the wars of the competing Roman generals. From the time of the Mithridatic wars to the final struggle with Antony they had been squeezed mercilessly. Sometimes they were forced into labor battalions by the thousand to help get supplies to the contending armies; armies are voracious things. The Roman soldiers, such as succeeded and survived, were rewarded fantastically at the expense of provincials (as well as of Romans unfortunate enough to be on the losing side). It is no surprise that provincials who at long last got peace eagerly accepted their deliverer as a species of deity.

Roman citizens, too, were glad to see the end. The support of the citizenry even at the expense of freedom to some degree was mostly due to exhaustion: exhaustion of men, of money, of land, of spirit. When Augustus wisely gave them a sop, the pretension of a restored republic, they extolled the regime and Augustus himself, as a superhuman saviour.

What did it matter that elections soon became mere formalities? That the popular juries were soon abolished? That the Senate became a rubber-stamp body? That the tribunician power protected the rights of the emperor more than the rights of the unprivileged? What did any of it matter, so there was peace and comfortable prosperity? Many did look back, but they did so more with nostalgia than with regret. The Romans accepted rather than made their bargain, but they did not find it so bad. And so the date 27 B.C.—a year when Augustus (as he was then named) announced the restoration of the Republic—is often cited as the year of the final demise of the Republic. Perhaps it had really been dead earlier; perhaps men like Caesar had alone perceived it. But now it was decently interred. The last rites were to continue to be celebrated for decades.

Part II

READINGS

— Reading No. 1 —

ITALY: AN ANCIENT ESTIMATION*

It is sometimes difficult to realize that by ancient Mediterranean standards Italy was rich in resources and manpower. This, more than may often be realized, helps to account for Rome's rise to power. The following passage is a Greek's view of Italy in the late first century B.C.

✓   ✓   ✓

I. 36. 3. Italy is, in my opinion, the best country, not only of Europe, but even of all the rest of the world. And yet I am not unaware that I shall not be believed by many when they reflect on Egypt, Libya, Babylonia and any other fertile countries there may be. But I, for my part, do not limit the wealth derived from the soil to one sort of produce, nor do I feel any eagerness to live where there are only rich arable lands and little or nothing else that is useful; but I account that country the best which is the most self-sufficient and generally stands least in need of imported commodities. And I am persuaded that Italy enjoys this universal fertility and diversity of advantages beyond any other land.

* Reprinted by permission of the publishers and The Loeb Classical Library from Dionysius Halicarnassus, *Roman Antiquities,* translated by E. Cary, Cambridge, Mass.: Harvard University Press, 1937.

37. For Italy does not, while possessing a great deal of good arable land, lack trees, as does a grain-bearing country; nor, on the other hand, while suitable for growing all manner of trees, does it, when sown to grain, produce scanty crops, as does a timbered country; nor yet, while yielding both grain and trees in abundance, is it unsuitable for the grazing of cattle; nor can anyone say that, while it bears rich produce of crops and timber and herds, it is nevertheless disagreeable for men to live in. Nay, on the contrary, it abounds in practically everything that affords either pleasure or profit.

To what grain-bearing country, indeed, watered, not with rivers, but with rains from heaven, do the plains of Campania yield, in which I have seen fields that produce even three crops in a year, summer's harvest following upon that of winter and autumn's upon that of summer? To what olive orchards are those of the Messapians, the Daunians, the Sabines and many others inferior? To what vineyards those of Tyrrhenia and the Alban and the Falernian districts, where the soil is wonderfully kind to vines and with the least labor produces the finest grapes in the greatest abundance? And besides the land that is cultivated one will find much that is left untilled as pasturage for sheep and goats, and still more extensive and more wonderful is the land suitable for grazing horses and cattle; for not only the marsh and meadow grass, which is very plentiful, but the dewy and well-watered grass of the glades, infinite in its abundance, furnish grazing for them in summer as well as in winter and keep them always in good condition.

But most wonderful of all are the forests growing upon the rocky heights, in the glens and on the uncultivated hills, from which the inhabitants are abundantly supplied with fine timber suitable for the building of ships as well as for all other purposes. Nor are any of these materials hard to come by or at a distance from human need, but they are easy to handle and readily available, owing to the multitude of rivers that flow through the whole peninsula and make the transportation and exchange of everything the land produces inexpensive. Springs also of hot water have been discovered in many places, affording most pleasant baths and sovereign cures for chronic ailments. There are also mines of all sorts, plenty of wild beasts for hunting, and a great variety of sea fish, besides innumerable other things, some useful and others of a nature to excite wonder.

But the finest thing of all is the climate, admirably tempered by the seasons, so that less than elsewhere is harm done by excessive cold or inordinate heat either to the growing fruits and grains or to the bodies of animals.

38. It is no wonder, therefore, that the ancients looked upon this country as sacred to Saturn. . . .

— Reading No. 2 —

THE ETRUSCANS

A. The Etruscans (or Tyrrhenians) as Immigrants*

The first paragraph of this passage probably derives from Herodotus. The second paragraph gives the essence of the literary tradition regarding the "Etruscan" kings of early Rome.

✓   ✓   ✓

V. 2. 2. The Tyrrheni have now received from the Romans the surname of Etrusci and Tusci. The Greeks thus named them from Tyrrhenus the son of Atys, as they say, who sent hither a colony from Lydia. Atys, who was one of the descendants of Hercules and Omphale, and had two sons, in a time of famine and scarcity determined by lot that Lydus should remain in the country, but that Tyrrhenus, with the greater part of the people, should depart. Arriving here, he named the country after himself, Tyrrhenia, and founded twelve cities, having appointed as their governor Tarcon, from whom the city of Tarquinia [received its name], and who, on account of

* From Strabo, *Geography,* translated by H. C. Hamilton (Bohn Classical Library), 1854.

the sagacity which he had displayed from childhood, was feigned to have been born with hoary hair. Placed originally under one authority they became flourishing; but it seems that in aftertimes, their confederation being broken up and each city separated, they yielded to the violence of the neighboring tribes. Otherwise they would never have abandoned a fertile country for a life of piracy on the sea, roving from one ocean to another; since, when united they were able not only to repel those who assailed them, but to act on the offensive, and undertake long campaigns.

After the foundation of Rome, Demaratus arrived here, bringing with him people from Corinth. He was received at Tarquinia, where he had a son, named Lucumo, by a woman of that country. Lucumo becoming the friend of Ancus Marcius, king of the Romans, succeeded him on the throne, and assumed the name of Lucius Tarquinius Priscus. Both he and his father did much for the embellishment of Tyrrhenia, the one by means of the numerous artists who had followed him from their native country; the other having the resources of Rome. It is said that the triumphal costume of the consuls, as well as that of the other magistrates, was introduced from the Tarquinii, with the fasces, axes, trumpets, sacrifices, divination, and music employed by the Romans in their public ceremonies. His son, the second Tarquin, named Superbus, who was driven from his throne, was the last king [of Rome]. Porsena, king of Clusium, a city of Tyrrhenia, endeavoured to replace him on the throne by force of arms, but not being able he made peace with the Romans, and departed in a friendly way, with honor and loaded with gifts.

B.   The Etruscans as Indigenous*

I. 27. But those who relate a legendary tale about their [Etruscans] having come from a foreign land say that Tyrrhenus, who was the leader of the colony, gave his name to the nation, and that he was a Lydian by birth, from the district formerly called Maeonia, and migrated in ancient times. They add that he was the fifth in descent

---

* Reprinted by permission of the publisher and The Loeb
  Classical Library from Dionysius Halicarnassus, *Roman
  Antiquities,* translated by E. Cary, Cambridge, Mass.:
  Harvard University Press, 1937.

from Zeus; for they say the son of Zeus and Ge was Manes, the first King of that country, and his son by Callirrhoe, the daughter of Oceanus, was Cotys, who by Halie, the daughter of earth-born Tyllus, had two sons, Asies and Atys, from the latter of whom by Callithea, the daughter of Choraeus, came Lydus and Tyrrhenus. Lydus, they continue, remaining there, inherited his father's kingdom, and from him the country was called Lydia; but Tyrrhenus, who was the leader of the colony, conquered a large portion of Italy and gave his name to those who had taken part in the expedition.

28. I am aware that many other authors also have given this account of the Tyrrhenian race, some in the same terms, and others changing the character of the colony and the date. For some have said that Tyrrhenus was the son of Herakles by Omphale, the Lydian, and that he, coming into Italy, dispossessed the Pelasgians of their cities, though not of all, but of these only that lay beyond the Tiber toward the north. Others declare that Tyrrhenus was the son of Telephus and that after the taking of Troy he came to Italy. But Xanthus of Lydia, who was as well acquainted with ancient history as any man and who may be regarded as an authority second to none on the history of his own country, neither names Tyrrhenus in any part of his history as a ruler of the Lydians nor knows anything of the landing of a colony of Maeonians in Italy; nor does he make the least mention of Tyrrhenia as a Lydian colony, though he takes notice of several things of less importance. He says that Lydus and Torebus were the sons of Atys; that they, having divided the kingdom they had inherited from their father, both remained in Asia, and from them the nations over which they reigned received their names. His words are these: "From Lydus are sprung the Lydians, and from Torebus the Torebians. There is little difference in their language and even now each nation scoffs at many words used by the other, even as do the Ionians and Dorians."

Hellanicus of Lesbos says that the Tyrrhenians, who were previously called Pelasgians, received their present name after they had settled in Italy. These are his words in the *Phoronis:* "Phrastor was the son of Pelasgus, their king, and Menippe, the daughter of Paneus; his son was Amyntor, Amyntor's son was Teutamides, and the latter's

son was Nanas. In his reign the Pelasgians were driven
out of their country by the Greeks, and after leaving their
ships on the river Spines in the Ionian Gulf, they took
Croton, an inland city; and proceeding from there, they
colonized the country now called Tyrrhenia." But the account Myrsilus gives is the reverse of that given by Hellanicus. The Tyrrhenians, he says, after they had left their
own country, were in the course of their wanderings called
Pelargoi or "Storks," from their resemblance to the birds
of that name, since they swarmed in flocks both into
Greece and into the barbarian lands; and they built the
wall round the citadel of Athens which is called the
Pelargic wall.

29. But in my opinion all who take the Tyrrhenians
and the Pelasgians to be one and the same nation are
mistaken. It is no wonder they were sometimes called by
one another's names, since the same thing has happened
to certain other nations also, both Greeks and barbarians
—for example, to the Trojans and Phrygians, who lived
near each other (indeed, many have thought that those
two nations were but one, differing in name only, not in
fact). And the nations in Italy have been confused under
a common name quite as often as any nations elsewhere.
For there was a time when the Latins, the Umbrians, the
Ausonians and many others were all called Tyrrhenians
by the Greeks, the remoteness of the countries inhabited
by these nations making their exact distinctions obscure to
those who lived at a distance. And many of the historians
have taken Rome itself for a Tyrrhenian city.

I am persuaded, therefore, that these nations changed
their name along with their place of abode, but cannot
believe that they both have a common origin, for this
reason, among many others, that their languages are different and preserve not the least resemblance to one another. "For neither the Crotoniats," says Herodotus, "nor
the Placians agree in language with any of their present
neighbors, although they agree with each other; and it is
clear that they preserve the fashion of speech which they
brought with them into those regions." However, one may
well marvel that, although the Crotoniats had a speech
similar to that of the Placians, who lived near the Hel-
lespont, since both were originally Pelasgians, it was not
at all similar to that of the Tyrrhenians, their nearest

neighbors. For if kinship is to be regarded as the reason why two nations speak the same language, the contrary must, of course, be the reason for their speaking a different one, since surely it is not possible to believe that both these conditions arise from the same cause. For, although it might reasonably happen, on the one hand, that men of the same nation who have settled at a distance from one another would, as the result of associating with their neighbors, no longer preserve the same fashion of speech, yet it is not at all reasonable that men sprung from the same race and living in the same country should not in the least agree with one another in their language.

30. For this reason, therefore, I am persuaded that the Pelasgians are a different people from the Tyrrhenians. And I do not believe, either, that the Tyrrhenians were a colony of the Lydians; for they do not use the same language as the latter, nor can it be alleged that, though they no longer speak a similar tongue, they still retain some other indications of their mother country. For they neither worship the same gods as the Lydians nor make use of similar laws or institutions, but in these very respects they differ more from the Lydians than from the Pelasgians. Indeed, those probably come nearest to the truth who declare that the nation migrated from nowhere else, but was a native of the country, since it is found to be a very ancient nation and to agree with no other either in its language or in its manner of living. And there is no reason why the Greeks should not have called them by this name, both from their living in towers and from the name of one of their rulers.

The Romans, however, give them other names: from the country they once inhabited, named Etruria, they call them Etruscans, and from their knowledge of the ceremonies relating to divine worship, in which they excel others, they now call them, rather inaccurately, Tusci, but formerly, with the same accuracy as the Greeks, they called them Thyoscoi. Their own name for themselves, however, is the same as that of one of their leaders, Rasenna.

— Reading No. 3 —

EARLY ROME

A. Research of the Late First Century B.C.*
Regarding the Chronology of Early Rome

I. 74. As to the last settlement or founding of the city, or whatever we ought to call it, Timaeus of Sicily, following what principle I do not know, places it at the same time as the founding of Carthage, that is, in the thirty-eighth year before the first Olympiad [*813 B.C.*]; Lucius Cincius, a member of the senate, places it about the fourth year of the twelfth Olympiad [*728 B.C.*], and Quintus Fabius in the first year of the eighth Olympiad [*747 B.C.*]. Porcius Cato does not give the time according to Greek reckoning, but being as careful as any writer in gathering the data of ancient history, he places its founding four hundred and thirty-two years after the Trojan war; and this time, being compared with the *Chronicles* of Eratosthenes, corresponds to the first year of the seventh Olympiad [*751 B.C.*]. That the canons of Eratosthenes are sound I have shown in another treatise, where I have also shown how the Roman chronology is to be synchronized with that of the Greeks. For I did not think it sufficient, like Polybius of Megalopolis, to say merely that I believe Rome was built in the second year of the seventh Olympiad [*750 B.C.*], nor to let my belief rest without further examination upon the single tablet preserved by the high priests, the only one of its kind, but I determined to set forth the reasons that had appealed to me, so that all might examine them who so desired.

* Reprinted by permission of the publisher and The Loeb Classical Library from Dionysius Halicarnassus, *Roman Antiquities,* translated by E. Cary, Cambridge, Mass.: Harvard University Press, 1937.

In that treatise, therefore, the detailed exposition is given; but in the course of the present work also the most essential of the conclusions there reached will be mentioned. The matter stands thus: It is generally agreed that the invasion of the Gauls, during which the city of Rome was taken, happened during the archonship of Pyrgion at Athens, in the first year of the ninety-eighth Olympiad [*387 B.C.*]. Now if the time before the taking of the city is reckoned back to Lucius Junius Brutus and Lucius Tarquinius Collatinus, the first consuls at Rome after the overthrow of the kings, it comprehends one hundred and twenty years. This is proved in many other ways, but particularly by the records of the censors, which the son received in succession from the father and takes great care to transmit to his posterity, like family rites; and there are many illustrious men of censorian families who preserve these records. In them I find that in the second year before the taking of the city there was a census of the Roman people, to which, as to the rest of them, there is affixed the date, as follows: "In the consulship of Lucius Valerius Potitus and Titus Manlius Capitolinus, in the one hundred and nineteenth year after the expulsion of the kings." So that the Gallic invasion, which we find to have occurred in the second year after the census, happened when the hundred and twenty years were completed. If, now, this interval of time is found to consist of thirty Olympiads, it must be allowed that the first consuls to be chosen entered upon their magistracy in the first year of the sixty-eighth Olympiad, the same year that Isagoras was archon at Athens [*507 B.C.*].

B. Early Days of the Republic*

Though Livy (who lived at the end of the Republic) and the other historians who wrote of the early Republic may not have left us a completely accurate account, nevertheless they have preserved what was over a long period considered significant. This reading will help to explain why, for example, Julius Caesar was hated by many because of the charge that he aimed at kingship.

✔   ✔   ✔

* From Livy, *From the Founding of the City,* translated by D. Spillan (Bohn Classical Library), 1886.

II. 1. The affairs, civil and military, of the Roman
people, henceforward free, their annual magistrates, and
the sovereignty of the laws, more powerful than that of
men, I shall now detail. The haughty insolence of the
late king [*Tarquin the Proud*] had caused this liberty to
be the more welcome; for the former kings reigned in
such a manner that they all in succession might be not
undeservedly set down as founders of the parts, at least
of the city, which they added as new residences for the
population augmented by themselves. Nor is there a doubt
but that the very same Brutus who earned so much glory
for expelling this haughty monarch, would have done so
to the greatest injury of the public weal, if, through an
over-hasty desire of liberty, he had wrested the kingdom
from any of the preceding kings. For what would have
been the consequence if that rabble of shepherds and
strangers, fugitives from their own countries, having,
under the protection of an inviolable asylum, found liberty, or at least impunity, uncontrolled by the dread of
regal authority, had begun to be distracted by tribunician
storms and to engage in contests with the fathers in a
strange city, before the pledges of wives and children,
and love of the very soil, to which it requires a length
of time to become habituated, had united their affections.
Their affairs not yet matured would have been destroyed
by discord, which the tranquil moderation of the government so cherished, and by proper nourishment brought
to such perfection, that, their strength being now developed, they were able to produce the wholesome fruits of
liberty. But the origin of liberty you may date from this
period, rather because the consular authority was made
annual, than that any diminution was made from the
kingly prerogative. The first consuls had all their privileges and ensigns of authority, only care was taken that
the terror might not appear doubled, by both having the
fasces at the same time. Brutus was, with the consent of
his colleague, first attended by the fasces, who had not
been a more zealous assertor of liberty than he was afterwards its guardian. First of all he bound over the people,
whilst still enraptured with their newly-acquired liberty,
by an oath . . . (2.) that they would suffer no one to
be king, nor any thing to be in Rome whence danger
might result to liberty.

C. Social Order: Patron and Client*

The following is perhaps the fullest description from antiquity of the client-patron system of early Rome. Since Dionysius was writing in the first century B.C., this account probably contains inaccuracies. But it seems at least fairly dependable and enlightening. It is very unlikely that Romulus or any other single person established the system by fiat.

✓ ✓ ✓

II. 10. The regulations which [*Romulus*] then instituted concerning patronage and which long continued in use among the Romans were as follows: It was the duty of the patricians to explain to their clients the laws, of which they were ignorant; to take the same care of them when absent as present, doing everything for them that fathers do for their sons with regard both to money and to the contracts that related to money; to bring suit on behalf of their clients when they were wronged in connexion with contracts, and to defend them against any who brought charges against them; and, to put the matter briefly, to secure for them both in private and in public affairs all that tranquillity of which they particularly stood in need.

It was the duty of the clients to assist their patrons in providing dowries for their daughters upon their marriage if the fathers had not sufficient means; to pay their ransom to the enemy if any of them or if their children were taken prisoner; to discharge out of their own purses their patrons' losses in private suits and the pecuniary fines which they were condemned to pay to the State, making these contributions to them not as loans but as thank-offerings; and to share with their patrons the costs incurred in their magistracies and dignities and other public expenditures, in the same manner as if they were their relations.

For both patrons and clients alike it was impious and unlawful to accuse each other in law-suits or to bear wit-

* Reprinted by permission of the publisher and The Loeb Classical Library from Dionysius Halicarnassus, *Roman Antiquities,* translated by E. Cary, Cambridge, Mass.: Harvard University Press, 1937.

ness or to give their votes against each other or to be
found in the number of each other's enemies; and whoever was convicted of doing any of these things was
guilty of treason by virtue of the law sanctioned by
Romulus, and might lawfully be put to death by any man
who so wished as a victim devoted to the Jupiter of the
infernal regions. For it was customary among the Romans, whenever they wished to put people to death without incurring any penalty, to devote their persons to some
god or other, and particularly to the gods of the lower
world; and this was the course which Romulus then
adopted. Accordingly, the connexions between the clients
and patrons continued for many generations, differing in
no wise from the ties of blood-relationship and being
handed down to their children's children.

And it was a matter of great praise to men of illustrious
families to have as many clients as possible and not only
to preserve the succession of hereditary patronages but
also by their own merit to acquire others. And it is incredible how great the contest of goodwill was between
the patrons and clients, as each side strove not to be outdone by the other in kindness, the clients feeling that they
should render all possible services to their patrons and
the patrons wishing by all means not to occasion any
trouble to their clients and accepting no gifts of money.
So superior was their manner of life to all pleasure; for
they measured their happiness by virtue, not by fortune.

11. It was not only in the city itself that the plebeians
were under the protection of the patricians, but every
colony of Rome and every city that had joined in alliance
and friendship with her and also every city conquered in
war had such protectors and patrons among the Romans
as they wished. And the senate has often referred the
controversies of these cities and nations to their Roman
patrons and regarded their decision as binding.

— Reading No. 4 —

EXPANSION: THE PUNIC WARS

A. Relations with Carthage Before the Wars*

Prior to the rather sudden outbreak of the First Punic War, Rome had maintained good relations with Carthage and had, in fact, three times concluded treaties of friendship with the African power. Polybius has preserved for us the exact wording of the treaties so far as he could. They represent, therefore, some of the oldest documentary evidence for Roman history—primary sources of a sort hard to come by. Some scholars believe the date of the first treaty was much later than that indicated (509/8 B.C.).

✓   ✓   ✓

1. TREATY OF 508 B.C.

III. 22. The first treaty between Rome and Carthage was made in the year of Lucius Junius Brutus and Marcus Horatius, the first consuls appointed after the expulsion of the kings, by which men also the temple of Jupiter Capitolinus was consecrated. This was twenty-eight years before the invasion of Greece by Xerxes. Of this treaty I append a translation, as accurate as I could make it,— for the fact is that the ancient language differs so much from that at present in use, that the best scholars among the Romans themselves have great difficulty in interpreting some points in it, even after much study. The treaty is as follows:

"There shall be friendship between the Romans and their allies, and the Carthaginians and their allies, on these conditions:

* From Polybius, *History,* translated by E. S. Shuckburgh (Bohn Classical Library), 1889.

"Neither the Romans nor their allies are to sail beyond the Fair Promontory, unless driven by stress of weather or the fear of enemies. If any one of them be driven ashore he shall not buy or take aught for himself save what is needful for the repair of his ship and the service of the gods, and he shall depart within five days.

"Men landing for traffic shall strike no bargain save in the presence of a herald or town-clerk. Whatever is sold in the presence of these, let the price be secured to the seller on the credit of the state—that is to say, if such sale be in Libya or Sardinia.

"If any Roman comes to the Carthaginian province in Sicily he shall enjoy all rights enjoyed by others. The Carthaginians shall do no injury to the people of Ardea, Antium, Laurentium, Circeii, Tarracina, nor any other people of the Latins that are subject to Rome.

"From those townships even which are not subject to Rome they shall hold their hands; and if they take one shall deliver it unharmed to the Romans. They shall build no fort in Latium; and if they enter the district in arms, they shall not stay a night therein."

2. SECOND TREATY

III. 24. After this treaty there was a second, in which we find that the Carthaginians have included the Tyrians and the township of Utica in addition to their former territory; and to the Fair Promontory Mastia and Tarseium are added, as the points east of which the Romans are not to make marauding expeditions or found a city. The treaty is as follows:

"There shall be friendship between the Romans and their allies and the Carthaginians, Tyrians, and the township of Utica, on these terms: The Romans shall not maraud, nor traffic, nor found a city east of the Fair Promontory, Mastia, Tarseium. If the Carthaginians take any city in Latium which is not subject to Rome, they may keep the prisoners and the goods, but shall deliver up the town. If the Carthaginians take any folk, between whom and Rome a peace has been made in writing, though they be not subject to them, they shall not bring them into any harbors of the Romans; if such an one be so brought ashore, and any Roman lay claim to him, he shall be released. In like manner shall the Romans be bound towards the Carthaginians.

"If a Roman take water or provisions from any district within the jurisdiction of Carthage, he shall not injure, while so doing, any between whom and Carthage there is peace and friendship. Neither shall a Carthaginian in like case. If anyone shall do so, he shall not be punished by private vengeance, but such action shall be a public misdemeanor.

"In Sardinia and Libya no Roman shall traffic nor found a city; he shall do no more than take in provisions and refit his ship. If a storm drive him upon those coasts, he shall depart within five days.

"In the Carthaginian province of Sicily and in Carthage he may transact business and sell whatsoever it is lawful for a citizen to do. In like manner also may a Carthaginian at Rome."

3. THIRD TREATY

III. 25. A third treaty again was made by Rome at the time of the invasion of Pyrrhus into Sicily; before the Carthaginians undertook war for the possession of Sicily [*i.e., for the possession of Messina just before the First Punic War.*] This treaty contains the same provisions as the two earlier treaties with these additional clauses:

"If they make a treaty of alliance with Pyrrhus, the Romans or Carthaginians shall make it on such terms as not to preclude the one giving aid to the other, if that one's territory is attacked.

"If one or the other stand in need of help, the Carthaginians shall supply the ships, whether for transport or war; but each people shall supply the pay for its own men employed on them.

"The Carthaginians shall also give aid by sea to the Romans if need be; but no one shall compel the crews to disembark against their will."

Provision was also made for swearing to these treaties. In the case of the first, the Carthaginians were to swear by the gods of their ancestors, the Romans by Jupiter Lapis, in accordance with an ancient custom; in the case of the last treaty, by Mars and Quirinus.

The form of swearing by Jupiter Lapis was this. The commissioner for swearing to the treaty took a stone in his hand, and, having taken the oath in the name of his country, added these words, "If I abide by this oath may he bless me; but if I do otherwise in thought or act, may all others be kept safe each in his own country, under his own laws, in enjoyment of his own goods, household gods, and tombs,—may I alone be cast out, even as this stone is now." And having uttered these words he throws the stone from his hand.

III. 26. Such treaties exist and are preserved to this day, engraved on brass in the treasury of the Aediles in the temple of Jupiter Capitolinus. . . .

B.   The Cunning of a Carthaginian (About 260 B.C.)*

Carthaginians gave severe treatment to unsuccessful generals, even executing some. The loser of the battle of Mylae—Rome's first victory at sea in the First Punic War —had no intention of losing his head.

✓   ✓   ✓

XXIII. 10. Hannibal [*grandfather of the great Hannibal?*], the general of the Carthaginians, having been defeated in a naval battle, and fearing that because of the defeat he might be punished by the [*Carthaginian*] senate, made use of the following artifice. He dispatched one of his friends to Carthage, and gave him such orders as seemed to him expedient. This man sailed home to the city, and when he had been brought before the senate said that Hannibal had ordered him to ask if it be the council's bidding that, with a fleet of two hundred ships, he should engage in battle with the Roman fleet of one hundred and twenty ships. With shouts of approval they urged him to give battle. "Very well," he said, "That is just why Hannibal did fight—and we have been beaten. But since you commanded it, he is relieved of the blame." Hannibal, then, knowing that his fellow citizens were wont to persecute their generals after the event, thus forestalled the accusations that were in the offing.

C.   Mercenaries—or Citizen-Soldiers?*

It is quite often alleged that one of the greatest weaknesses of Carthage as compared to Rome was her dependence on mercenary troops. To a degree this was true —but only because Rome had available such immense (by ancient standards) reserves of manpower. The other side of the story is told well by Diodorus.

* Reprinted by permission of the publisher and The Loeb Classical Library from Diodorus of Sicily, *Universal History,* translated by F. R. Walton, Cambridge, Mass.: Harvard University Press, 1957.

1   *1*   *1*

XXIX. 6. In warfare a ready supply of money is indeed, as the familiar proverb has it, the sister of success, since he who is well provided with money never lacks men able to fight. So, for example, the Carthaginians recently brought the Romans to the brink of disaster, yet it was not with an army of citizens that they won their victories in those great engagements, but by the great number of their mercenary soldiers. An abundance of foreign troops is, in fact, very advantageous to the side that employs them, and very formidable to the enemy, inasmuch as the employers bring together at trifling cost men to do battle in their behalf, while citizen soldiers, even if victorious, are nevertheless promptly faced with a fresh crop of opponents. In the case of citizen armies, a single defeat spells complete disaster [*Diodorus here must be thinking of the smaller Greek city-states*], but in the case of mercenaries, however many times they suffer defeat, none the less the employers maintain their forces intact as long as their money lasts. It is not however, the custom of the Romans to employ mercenaries, nor have they sufficient resources.

D. Treaty Between Hannibal and King Philip V of Macedon, 215 B.C.*

VII. 9. This is a sworn treaty made between Hannibal, Mago, Barmocarus, and such members of the Carthaginian Gerusia as were present, and all Carthaginians serving in his army, on the one part; and Xenophanes, son of Cleomachus of Athens, sent to us by King Philip, as his ambassador, on behalf of himself, the Macedonians, and their allies, on the other part.

The oath is taken in the presence of Zeus, Here, and Apollo: of the god of the Carthaginians, Hercules, and Iolaus: of Ares, Triton, Poseidon: of the gods that accompany the army, and of the sun, moon, and earth: of rivers, harbors, waters: of all the gods who rule Carthage: of all the gods who rule Macedonia and the rest of Greece: of all the gods of war that are witnesses to this oath.

* From Polybius, *op. cit.*

Hannibal, general, and all the Carthaginian senators with him, and all Carthaginians serving in his army, subject to our mutual consent, proposes to make this sworn treaty of friendship and honorable good-will. Let us be friends, close allies, and brethren, on the conditions herein following:

(1) Let the Carthaginians, as supreme, Hannibal their chief general and those serving with him, all members of the Carthaginian dominion living under the same laws, as well as the people of Utica, and the cities and tribes subject to Carthage, and their soldiers and allies, and all cities and tribes in Italy, Celt-land, and Liguria, with whom we have a compact of friendship, and with whomsoever in this country we may hereafter form such compact, be supported by King Philip and the Macedonians, and all other Greeks in alliance with them.

(2) On their parts also King Philip and the Macedonians, and such other Greeks as are his allies, shall be supported and protected by the Carthaginians now in this army, and by the people of Utica, and by all cities and tribes subject to Carthage, both soldiers and allies, and by all allied cities and tribes in Italy, Celt-land, and Liguria, and by all others in Italy as shall hereafter become allies of the Carthaginians.

(3) We will not make plots against, nor lie in ambush for, each other; but in all sincerity and good will, without reserve or secret design, will be enemies to the enemies of the Carthaginians, saving and excepting those kings, cities, and ports with which we have sworn agreements and friendships.

(4) And we, too, will be enemies to the enemies of King Philip, saving and excepting those kings, cities, and tribes, with which we have sworn agreements and friendships.

(5) Ye shall be friends to us in the war in which we now are engaged against the Romans, till such time as the gods give us and you the victory: and ye shall assist us in all ways that be needful, and in whatsoever way we may mutually determine.

(6) And when the gods have given us victory in our war with the Romans and their allies, if Hannibal shall deem it right to make terms with the Romans, these terms shall include the same friendship with you, made on these

conditions: (1) the Romans not to be allowed to make war on you; (2) not to have power over Corcyra, Apollonia, Epidamnum, Pharos, Dimale, Parthini, nor Atitania; (3) to restore to Demetrius of Pharos all those of his friends now in the dominion of Rome.

(7) If the Romans ever make war on you or on us we will aid each other in such war, according to the need of either.

(8) So also if any other nation whatever does so, always excepting kings, cities, and tribes, with whom we have sworn agreements and friendships.

(9) If we decide to take away from, or add to this sworn treaty, we will so take away, or add thereto, only as we both may agree.

E. Rome Refuses to Ransom Prisoners after Cannae*

This reading helps to show why the Romans were men of stern fiber.

✓   ✓   ✓

VI. 58. When Hannibal, after conquering the Romans in the battle at Cannae, got possession of the eight thousand who were guarding the Roman camp, he made them all prisoners of war, and granted them permission to send messages to their relations that they might be ransomed and return home. They accordingly selected ten of their chief men, whom Hannibal allowed to depart after binding them with an oath to return. . . . Upon the arrival of the envoys at Rome, imploring and beseeching the Senate not to grudge the captured troops their return home, but to allow them to rejoin their friends by paying three minae each for them—for these were the terms, they said, granted by Hannibal—and declaring that the men deserved redemption, for they had neither played the coward in the field, nor done anything unworthy of Rome, but had been left behind to guard the camp; and that, when all the rest had perished, they had yielded to absolute necessity in surrendering to Hannibal: though the Romans had been severely defeated in the battles, and though they were at the time deprived of, roughly speak-

* Ibid.

ing all their allies, they neither yielded so far to misfortune as to disregard what was becoming to themselves, nor omitted to take into account any necessary consideration. They saw through Hannibal's purpose in thus acting—which was at once to get a large supply of money, and at the same time to take away all enthusiasm from the troops opposed to him, by showing that even the conquered had a hope of getting safe home again. Therefore the Senate, far from acceding to the request, refused all pity even to their own relations, and disregarded the services to be expected from these men in the future: and thus frustrated Hannibal's calculations, and the hopes which he had founded on these prisoners, by refusing to ransom them; and at the same time established the rule for their own men, that they must either conquer or die on the field, as there was no other hope of safety for them if they were beaten.

F. Hannibal at the Gates of Rome, 211 B.C.*

Hannibal had little chance of taking Rome itself unless he could either break up the Roman alliance system in central Italy or receive substantial reinforcements from Carthage. Neither of these things happened. At one point, nevertheless, in order to try to relieve the Roman siege of rebel Capua, he marched on Rome. Despite the statements made here, it is doubtful if Hannibal hoped for anything more than to cause the Romans to recall a portion of the Roman army before Capua—which he might ambush along the way.

✓ ✓ ✓

IX. 5. [*Hannibal*] took the road through Samnium, and marched at a great pace and without stopping, his skirmishers always keeping before him to reconnoitre and occupy all the posts along the route: and while those in Rome had their thoughts still wholly occupied with Capua and the campaign there, he crossed the Anio without being observed; and having arrived at a distance of not more than forty stades from Rome, there pitched his camp.

6. On this being known at Rome, the utmost confusion and terror prevailed among the inhabitants—this move-

* *Ibid.*

ment of Hannibal's being as unexpected as it was sudden; for he had never been so close to the city before. At the same time their alarm was increased by the idea at once occurring to them, that he would not have ventured so near, if it were not that the armies at Capua were destroyed. Accordingly, the men at once went to line the walls, and the points of vantage in the defenses of the town; while the women went round to the temples of the gods and implored their protection, sweeping the pavements of the temples with their hair: for this is their customary way of behaving when any serious danger comes upon their country. But just as Hannibal had encamped, and was intending to attempt the city itself next day, an extraordinary coincidence occurred which proved fortunate for the preservation of Rome.

For Gnaeus Fulvius and Publius Sulpicius, having already enrolled one consular army [*two legions*], had bound the men with the usual oath to appear at Rome armed on that very day: and were also engaged on that day in drawing out the lists and testing the men for the other army: whereby it so happened that a large number of men had been collected in Rome spontaneously in the very nick of time. These troops the consuls boldly led outside the walls, and, entrenching themselves there, checked Hannibal's intended movement. For the Carthaginians were at first eager to advance, and were not altogether without hope that they would be able to take Rome itself by assault. But when they saw the enemy drawn up in order, and learnt before long from a prisoner what had happened, they abandoned the idea of attacking the city, and began devastating the countryside instead, and setting fire to the houses. In these first raids they collected an innumerable amount of booty, for the field of plunder upon which they were entered was one into which no one had ever expected an enemy to set foot.

LATIN AND ITALIAN RELATIONS WITH ROME

A. Migrations to the Cities Weaken Allied Armies, 177 B.C.*

With the expansion of Rome the privileges of Roman citizenship became relatively greater for persons of all classes. Large numbers of Latins and Italians from states whose treaties with Rome permitted them to become citizens of that state removed to Rome, with consequent problems for the states which had to furnish quotas for auxiliary service in the Roman army.

✔   ✔   ✔

XLI. 8. Ambassadors from the confederate states of Latium, who, after having ineffectually applied to the former consuls and censors, were at last introduced to an audience, made a powerful impression on the senate. The amount of their complaints was, that "their citizens, having been rated in the general survey [*census*] at Rome, had most of them removed thither; and that if this practice were allowed, it would come to pass, in the course of a very few lustrums [*census periods, about five years*], that their deserted towns and country would be unable to furnish any soldiers." The Samnites and the Pelignians also represented, that four thousand families had emigrated to Fregellae; and that neither of these places furnished less soldiers on that account. That there had been practiced two species of fraud in individuals changing their citizenship: there was a law which granted liberty to any of the allies or Latins to be enrolled a citizen of

* From Livy, *op. cit.* (this section translated by W. A. M'Devitte).

Rome who should leave his offspring at home; yet, by an abuse of this law, some did injury to the allies, others to the Roman people. For at first, to evade the leaving offspring at home, they made over their children as slaves to some Roman, under an agreement that they should be again set free, and thus become citizens by emancipation; and then those men, who had now no children to leave, became Roman citizens. Afterwards, they neglected even these appearances of law; and, without any regard either to the ordinances or to progeny, passed indiscriminately into the Roman state by migration, and getting themselves included in the survey. To prevent such proceedings in the future, the ambassadors requested the senate to order the allies to return to their respective states, and to provide by a law that no one should make any man his property, or alienate such property for the purpose of a change of citizenship; and that if any person should by such means be made a citizen of Rome, he should not enjoy the rights of a citizen."

9. The senate granted their petitions. . . . Caius Claudius, by direction of the senate, proposed a law and issued a proclamation, that "any of the allies and Latin confederates, who themselves, or whose ancestors, had been surveyed among the associated states of Latium in the censorship of Marcus Claudius and Titus Quintius [189 B.C.], or at any time since, should all return, each to his respective state, before the calends of November." Inquiry concerning such as did not obey, was intrusted to Lucius Mummius the praetor. To the law and the proclamation of the consul, was added a decree of the senate that "the dictator, consul, interrex, censor, or praetor, who then should be in office, before whom any slave should be brought to receive manumission, should cause the said slave who was about to be made free to make oath that the person giving him liberty did not do it for the purpose of his changing his citizenship. . . ."

B. Encroachment on Allied Rights by Roman Magistrates, 174-173 B.C.*

The growing importance of Rome during the period of expansion meant that the relative position of her Latin

* Ibid.

and Italian allies tended to shrink. Certain Roman magis-
trates, further, abused their positions and damaged the
relationship with her allies. Perhaps the two incidents re-
lated below are isolated, but even isolated incidents can
become symbols to persons who consider themselves mis-
treated.

✔   ✔   ✔

XLII. 1. The senate resolved that . . . Lucius Postu-
mius should go into Campania, to fix the bounds between
the lands which were private property and those which
belonged to the public; for it was understood that individuals, by gradually extending their bounds, had taken
possession of a very considerable share of the common
lands [*ager publicus*]. He, being enraged with the people
of Praeneste because, when he had gone thither as a
private individual to offer sacrifice in the temple of Fortune, no honor had been paid him, either in public or
private, by the people of Praeneste, before he set out
from Rome, sent a letter to Praeneste, ordering the chief
magistrate to meet him, and to provide him lodging at
the public expense; and that, at his departure, cattle should
be ready to carry his baggage.

No consul before him ever put the allies to any trouble
or expense whatever. Magistrates were furnished with
mules, tents, and every other requisite for a campaign, in
order that they might not make any such demands. They
had private lodgings, in which they behaved with courtesy
and kindness, and their houses at Rome were always open
to their hosts with whom they used to lodge. Ambassadors
indeed sent to any place, on a sudden emergency, demanded each a single horse in the several towns through
which their journey lay; but the allies never contributed
any other portion of the expense of the Roman magistrates. The resentment of the consul, which, even if well
founded, ought not to have been exerted during his office,
and the too modest or too timid acquiescence of the
Praenestines, gave to the magistrates, as if by an approved
precedent, the privilege of imposing orders of this sort,
which grew more burdensome daily.

XLII. 3. In the same year, the temple of Juno Lacinia
was uncovered. Quintus Fulvius Flaccus, the censor, was
erecting a temple to Equestrian Fortune, which he had

vowed when praetor during the Celtiberian war, with anxious desire that it should not be surpassed by any other at Rome, either in size or magnificence. Thinking that he would add a very great ornament to this temple if the tiles were marble, he went to Bruttium and stripped off about the half of those belonging to the temple of the Lacinian Juno; for he computed that so many would be sufficient to cover the one he was building. Ships were in readiness to take on board the materials, while the allies were deterred by the authority of the censor from preventing the sacrilege. When the censor returned, the marble was landed and carried to the temple; but though he made no mention of the place from which it was brought, yet such an affair could not be concealed. Accordingly, considerable murmuring arose in the senate; from all sides of the house a demand was made that the consuls should lay that matter before the senate. When the censor, on being summoned, appeared in the senate-house, they all, both separately and in a body, inveighed against him with great asperity. . . . When the question was put, they unanimously concurred in voting, that a contract should be entered into for carrying the tiles back to the temple, and that atonements should be offered to Juno. What regarded the atonements was carefully executed; the contractors made a report that they were obliged to leave the marble in the court of the temple, because no workman could be found who knew how to replace the same.

— Reading No. 6 —

THE ROMAN RULING CLASS

A. Occupations Suitable for the Roman Aristocrat*

As a new man Cicero was never really accepted by the Roman nobility. But he adhered largely to aristocratic standards, as this passage shows.

✓ ✓ ✓

I. 42. Now with regard to what arts and means of acquiring wealth [*for the senatorial aristocracy*] are to be regarded as worthy and what disreputable, we have been taught as follows. In the first place, those sources of emolument are condemned that incur the public hatred; such as those of tax-gatherers and usurers. We are likewise to account as ungenteel and mean the gains of all hired workmen, whose source of profit is not their art but their labor; for their very wages are the consideration of their servitude. We are likewise to despise all who retail from merchants goods for prompt sale; for they never can succeed unless they lie most abominably. Now nothing is more disgraceful than insincerity. All mechanical laborers are by their profession mean. For a workship can contain nothing befitting a gentleman. Least of all are those trades to be approved that serve the purposes of sensuality, such as (to speak after Terence) fishmongers, butchers, cooks, pastry-cooks, and fishermen; to whom we shall add, if you please, perfumers, dancers, and the whole tribe of gamesters.

But those professions that involve a higher degree of intelligence or a greater amount of utility, such as medi-

* From Cicero, *On the Offices,* translated by C. R. Edmonds (Harper's Classical Library), 1855.

cine, architecture, the teaching the liberal arts, are honorable in those to whose rank in life they are suited. As to merchandizing, if on a small scale it is mean; but if it is extensive and rich, bringing numerous commodities from all parts of the world, and giving bread to numbers without fraud, it is not so despicable. But if a merchant, satiated, or rather satisfied with his profits, as he sometimes used to leave the open sea and make the harbor, shall from the harbor step into an estate and lands; such a man seems most justly deserving of praise. For of all gainful professions, nothing is better, nothing more pleasing, nothing more delightful, nothing better becomes a well-bred man than agriculture.

B. Public Funerals of Ranking Nobles*

The following description of the funeral of a Roman aristocrat of note in Polybius' time (middle second century B.C.) helps to underscore the Roman attachment to the mos maiorum—*customs of the ancestors. The recitation, often repeated, of ancestral deeds, no doubt preserved a great many stories which have been enshrined in the histories of Rome both ancient and modern. The historian must, of course, be aware of the possibility of embellishment or even fabrication, through family pride. This passage also helps us to understand the later Roman emphasis upon portrait sculpture.*

✓   ✓   ✓

VI. 53. Whenever one of their illustrious men dies, in the course of his funeral, the body with all its paraphernalia is carried into the forum to the Rostra, as a raised platform there is called, and sometimes is propped upright upon it so as to be conspicuous, or, more rarely, is laid upon it. Then with all the people standing round, his son, if he has left one of full age and he is there, or, failing him, one of his relations, mounts the Rostra and delivers a speech concerning the virtues of the deceased, and the successful exploits performed by him in his lifetime. By these means the people are reminded of what has been done, and made to see it with their own eyes—

* From Polybius, *op. cit.*

not only such as were engaged in the actual transactions but those also who were not—and their sympathies are so deeply moved, that the loss appears not to be confined to the actual mourners, but to be a public one affecting the whole people.

After the burial and all the usual ceremonies have been performed, they place the likeness of the deceased in the most conspicuous spot in his house, surmounted by a wooden canopy or shrine. This likeness consists of a mask made to represent the deceased with extraordinary fidelity both in shape and color. These likenesses they display at public sacrifices adorned with much care. And when any illustrious member of the family dies, they carry these masks to the funeral, putting them on men whom they thought as like the originals as possible in height and other personal peculiarities. And these substitutes assume clothes according to the rank of the person represented: if he was a consul or praetor, a toga with purple stripes; if a censor, whole purple; if he had also celebrated a triumph or performed any exploit of that kind, a toga embroidered with gold. These representatives also ride themselves in chariots, while the fasces and axes, and all the other customary insignia of the particular offices lead the way, according to the dignity of the rank in the state enjoyed by the deceased in his lifetime; their seats on ivory chairs in their order. There could not easily be a more inspiring spectacle than this for a young man of noble ambitions and virtuous aspirations. For can we conceive any one to be unmoved at the sight of all the likenesses collected together of the men who have earned glory, all as it were living and breathing? Or what could be a more glorious spectacle?

VI. 54. The speaker over the body about to be buried, after having finished the panegyric of this particular person, starts upon the others whose representatives are present, beginning with the most ancient, and recounts the successes and achievements of each. By this means the glorious memory of brave men is continually renewed; the fame of those who have performed any noble deed is never allowed to die; and the renown of those who have done good service to their country becomes a matter of common knowledge to the multitude, and part of the heritage of posterity.

C.   Factional In-Fighting Among the Nobles*

This reading illustrates how religious rites served (probably) as a pretext to achieve a political purpose. The action here resulted in the resignation of two consuls of an opposing family faction and the election of other persons. The evidence for these factions among the nobility is not specifically described in any ancient author and has been inferred by modern scholars.

✓   ✓   ✓

II. 4. He [*Tiberius Gracchus, father of the famous tribunes*] wrote from his province to the college of augurs, acknowledging that in reading the books he remembered that he had illegally chosen a place for his tent in the gardens of Scipio, and had afterwards entered the Pomoerium, in order to hold a senate, that in repassing the same Pomoerium he had forgotten to take the auspices; and that, therefore, the consuls had been created informally. The augurs laid the case before the senate. The senate decreed that they should resign their charge, and so they accordingly abdicated.

— Reading No. 7 —

CHANGING SOCIETY IN THE SECOND CENTURY B.C.

A.   Roman Small Farmers Appeal Long Military Service, 171 B.C.†

The numerous wars, especially in the period 219 B.C.- 146 B.C., put great demands on the Roman small farmers. When preparations were under way for the war

* From Cicero, *On the Nature of the Gods,* translated by
    C. D. Yonge (Bohn Classical Library), 1902.
† From Livy, *op. cit.*

against Perseus, some veterans who felt they had served long enough—many longer than was legally demanded of them—announced they would appeal the draft. The speech reproduced below (if Livy has correctly reported it) caused them to change their minds. It also indicates what a burden military service might be in this period. Of course it should be recalled that many Romans profited in these wars and indeed preferred military service (or life in Rome) to the hard work that a small farm operation entailed.

✓   ✓   ✓

XLII. 34. Spurius Ligustinus, one of those who had appealed to the plebeian tribunes, requested permission from the consul and tribunes to speak a few words to the people. By the permission of them all he spoke, we are told, to this effect: "Romans, I am Spurius Ligustinus, of the Crustuminian tribe, and sprung from the Sabines. My father left me one acre of land, and a small cottage, in which I was born and educated, and I dwell there today. As soon as I came to man's estate, my father married me to his brother's daughter, who brought nothing with her but independence and modesty; except, indeed, a degree of fruitfulness that would have better suited a wealthier family. We have six sons and two daughters; the latter are both married; of our sons, four are grown up to manhood, the other two are as yet boys.

"I became a soldier in the consulate of Publius Sulpicius and Caius Aurelius [*200 B.C.*]. In the army which was sent over into Macedon I served as a common soldier, against Philip, for two years; and in the third year, Titus Quintius [*sic*] Flamininus, in reward of my good conduct, gave me the command of the tenth company of spearmen. When Philip and the Macedonians were subdued, and we were brought back to Italy and discharged, I immediately went as a volunteer, with the consul Marcus Porcius [*Cato*] into Spain. Those who have had experience of him, and of other generals in a long course of service, know that no single commander living was a more accurate observer and judge of merit. This commander judged me deserving of being set at the head of the first company of spearmen. A third time I entered as a volunteer in the army which was sent against the Aetolians and King

Antiochus; and Manius Acilius gave me the command of the first company of first-rank men. After Antiochus was driven out of the country, and the Aetolians were reduced, we were brought home to Italy, where I served the two succeeding years in legions that were raised annually. I afterwards made two campaigns in Spain; one under Quintus Fulvius Flaccus, the other under Tiberius Sempronius Gracchus, praetors. I was brought home from the province to attend his triumph, out of regard to their good services. At the request of Tiberius Gracchus, I went with him to his province. Four times within a few years was I first centurion of my corps; thirty-four times I was honored by my commanders with presents for bravery. I have received six civic crowns, I have fulfilled twenty-two years of service in the army, and I am upwards of fifty years of age." (Nevertheless Ligustinus was willing to serve and persuaded the others to drop their appeals. He was rewarded by being made the first centurion of the first legion.)

B. The Comedy-Playwrights' Concessions to the Mos Maiorum (Early Second Century B.C.)

Plautus (254-184 B.C.) was Rome's ranking comic playwright. His are the earliest complete literary works remaining. He borrowed from the Hellenistic Greek playwrights and adapted them to suit Roman conditions. The changes are especially interesting to historians as implying certain social, economic, or other conditions at Rome. The evaluation of these works for history is difficult but rewarding.

Generally Plautus's humor was coarse; he does not often display serious purpose. The following passages are not, therefore, typical; but they may be enlightening in some fashion. It is well to remember that comedians sometimes exaggerate.

✓   ✓   ✓

1.*

"Attend to me this day; good things I bring upon the stage; for I think 'tis very just that to the good good things should be brought; as likewise bad things to the

* From Plautus, *The Cheat,* translated by H. T. Riley (Bohn Classical Library), 1852.

bad; that those who are bad may have what's bad, those
who are good what's good; bad men are bad because they
hate the good; because the good condemn the bad, needs
must be that they are good; and therefore, you are good
since you have ever abhorred the bad; and both by your
laws, Quirites, and by your legions have you routed them
with good success."

2.*

"Really it will be worth your while to give your attention to this play. 'Tis not composed in the hackneyed
style, nor yet like other plays, nor are there in it any
ribald lines unfit for utterance: here is neither the perjured procurer, nor the artful courtesan, nor yet the brag-
gart captain."

*   *   *

"Spectators, this play is founded on chaste manners.
No wenching is there in this, and no intriguing, no exposure of a child, no cheating out of money; and no young
man in love here makes his mistress free without his
father's knowledge. The Poets find but few Comedies [*i.e.,
from earlier Greek playwrights*] of this kind, where good
men might become better. Now, if it pleases you, and if
we have pleased you, and have not been tedious, do you
give this sign of it: you who wish that chaste manners
should have their reward, give us your applause."

3.†

"He who desires to meet with a perjured fellow, let him
go into the courts of law; he who wants a liar and a brag-
gart, near the rites of Cloacina. The rich and erring husbands seek you at the magisterial halls of the Basilica.
There, too, will be the worn-out harlots, and those who
are wont to haggle for them. Contributors to the picnic
dinners you'll find in the fishmarket. In the lower part of
the Forum good men and opulent do walk; in the middle,
near the canal, there are the mere puffers-off. Beyond the

* From Plautus, *The Captives,* translated by H. T. Riley
    (Bohn Classical Library), 1852.
† From Plautus, *The Forgery,* translated by H. T. Riley
    (Bohn Classical Library), 1852.

lake of Curtius are impudent, talkative, and malevolent fellows, who boldly, without reason, utter calumnies about another, and who, themselves, have sufficient that might with truth be said against them. There, at the old shops, are those who lend and those who borrow at interest. Behind the Temple of Castor there are those to whom unguardedly you may be lending to your cost. There, in the Etrurian street, are those men who hold themselves on sale. In the Velabrum you'll find either baker, or butcher, or soothsayer; either those who sell retail themselves, or supply to others things to be sold by retail. Rich sinning husbands you'll find at the house of Oppian Leucadia."

*   *   *

"My clever one-eyed friend . . . you are well acquainted with the Procurers."

"You bankers . . . I put and place in the same rank; you are the very counterparts of them. They, at least, are on sale in dark corners, you in the very Forum. You tear men to pieces with usury, they by persuading them amiss and by means of their dens. Full many a proposed statute has the public confirmed on your account, which when confirmed you break; some loophole you find out; just as boiling water becomes cold, so do you deem the laws."

C. Bringing Up Children: Permissiveness or Discipline?*

Terence (c. 185-159 B.C.) was associated with the younger Scipio and the group of phil-Hellene intellectuals known as the "Scipionic Circle." Romans of the old school like the elder Cato looked askance at the new learning, fearing that the looser morals of the Greeks might come in with Greek culture.

Terence's Adelphi (The Brothers), adapted as usual from a Greek play, seemed to the most conservative Romans to justify their worst fears. Terence himself, in the prologue, tells us that "his adversaries represent in a bad light the play that we (actors) are about to perform." The play attacks, somewhat subtly, the overly stern discipline of the rural Roman and advocates a "permissive"

* From Terence, *The Brothers*, translated by H. T. Riley (Bohn Classical Library), 1868.

and reasonable approach in the training of young men.
In view of the current worry over rising youthful delin-
quency and over the feared lack of discipline within the
family in 20th-century America, the play has an almost
contemporary tone.

The plot concerns itself with two brothers, one stern,
the other permissive, each of whom brought up one son
of the stern brother. The son brought up by the permissive
methods turned out to have the higher character.

The play was performed at the funeral of Lucius
Aemilius Paullus, victor of Pydna, who was himself a
stern disciplinarian in the army, at least. It was put on by
his two sons, Q. Fabius Maximus and P. Cornelius Scipio
(both Aemilianus, of course). This excerpt, from the first
scene of the first act, is the introductory speech of the
brother who relies on gentler methods.

1   1   1

MICIO: "I, from my very youth upwards, have lived a
comfortable town life, and taken my ease; and what they
esteem a piece of luck, I have never had a wife. He
[*Demea, his brother*] married a wife, and has two sons.
This one, the elder of them, I have adopted. I have
brought him up from an infant, and considered and loved
him as my own. In him I centre my delight; this object
alone is dear to me. On the other hand, I take all due care
that he may hold me equally dear. I give—I overlook; I
do not judge it necessary to exert my authority in everything; in fine, the things that youth prompts to, and that
others do unknown to their fathers, I have used my son
not to conceal from me. For he, who, as the practice is,
will dare to tell a lie to or to deceive his father, will still
more dare to do so to others. I think it better to restrain
children through a sense of shame and liberal treatment,
than through fear.

"On these points my brother does not agree with me,
nor do they please him. He often comes to me exclaiming,
'What are you about, Micio? Why do you ruin for us
this youth? Why does he intrigue? Why does he drink?
Why do you supply him with the means for these goings
on? You indulge him with too much dress; you are very
inconsiderate.' He himself is too strict, beyond what is

just and reasonable; and he is very much mistaken, in my opinion, at all events, who thinks that an authority is more firm or more lasting which is established by force, than that which is founded on affection.

"Such is my mode of reasoning; and thus do I persuade myself. He who, compelled by harsh treatment, does his duty, so long as he thinks it will be known, is on his guard: if he hopes that it will be concealed, he again returns to his natural bent. He whom you have secured by kindness, acts from inclination; he is anxious to return like for like; present and absent, he will be the same. This is the duty of a parent, to accustom a son to do what is right rather of his own choice, than through fear of another. In this the father differs from the master: he who cannot do this, let him confess that he does not know how to govern children."

*   *   *

"Does he feast, does he drink, does he smell of perfumes—it is at my cost. Does he intrigue, money shall be found by me, so long as it suits me; when it shall be no longer convenient, probably he'll be shut out of doors. Has he broken open a door—it shall be replaced; has he torn any one's clothes—they shall be mended. Thanks to the Gods, I both have means for doing this, and these things are not as yet an annoyance."

DEMEA: (in act V, after discovering that his rigid discipline had not worked so well after all) "Never was there any person of ever such well-trained habits of life, but that experience, age, and custom are always bringing him something new or suggesting something; so much so that what you have fancied of first importance to you, on making trial you reject; and this is my case at present: for the rigid life I have hitherto led, my race nearly run, I now renounce. Why so? I have found, by experience, that there is nothing better for a man than an easy temper and complacency. . . . Well, then, henceforward let us try, on the other hand, whether I can't speak kindly and act complaisantly. . . . I also want myself to be loved and highly valued by my friends. If that is to be effected by giving and indulging, I will not be behind him."

(It should be added that Demea then goes on to overdo

his newly acquired generosity—especially at the expense
of his brother—and so the point is made that society
would go to pieces if everyone were indulgent and no one
left to reprove.)

— Reading No. 8 —

RELIGION AND THE AUSPICES

A. Religion a Part of the State—The Mos Maiorum

*Religion at Rome was less a set of beliefs than a set of
practices. To adhere to the customs of the ancestors in
the state religion was for the Roman a matter of simple
patriotism.*

*The introduction of skepticism at Rome after about
mid-second century B.C., along with Greek learning, may
have produced some weakening of the state religion. The
changing population of Rome in the last two centuries of
the Republic brought the introduction of new religions
and may also have resulted in the weakening of the ties
of state religion, eventually even in the neglect of priest-
hoods and temples.*

*It is easily understood that the more conservative Ro-
mans, especially, that is, the* optimates, *deplored these
tendencies. Some of the popular leaders seem to have supported the newer religions. This would of course intensify
the efforts of the* optimates, *who saw any attack on traditional religion as contributing to the decline of the Republic as they conceived it.*

These passages illustrate optimate *views.*

🖋   🖋   🖋

1.*

This oration was given by Cicero before the college of fifteen pontiffs, headed by the pontifex maximus, soon after his return from exile.

✓   ✓   ✓

I. Many things, O priests, have been devised and established with divine wisdom by our ancestors; but no action of theirs was ever more wise than their determination that the same men should superintend both what relates to the religious worship due to the immortal gods, and also what concerns the highest interests of the state, so that they might preserve the republic as the most honorable and eminent of the citizens, by governing it well, and as priests by wisely interpreting the requirements of religion. [*Roman priests were lay priests, chosen from the governing classes.*]

2.†

This oration came soon after the preceding one. Cicero supported the Soothsayers who argued the current neglect of the gods.

✓   ✓   ✓

IX. Let us, O conscript fathers [*senators*], think as highly of ourselves as we please; and yet it is not in numbers that we are superior to the Spaniards, nor in personal strength to the Gauls, nor in cunning to the Carthaginians, nor in arts to the Greeks, nor in the natural acuteness, which seems to be implanted in the people of this land and country, to the Italian and Latin tribes; but it is in and by means of piety and religion, and this especial wisdom of perceiving that all things are governed and managed by the divine power of the immortal gods, that we have been and are superior to all other countries and nations.

* From Cicero, *Oration on His Own House,* translated by C. D. Yonge (Bohn Classical Library), 1886.
† From Cicero, *Oration Respecting the Answers of the Soothsayers,* translated by C. D. Yonge (Bohn Classical Library), 1886.

B.   Religious Tales of a Moral Nature*

Cicero himself was relatively enlightened and not super-stitious, although his reverence for ancestral custom could make him almost a believer. His recounting of the stories in the first two readings below serve to show us not his own attitude, but the stories earlier Romans told of the dire consequences of ignoring the auspices. He points out, in a section of the De Divinatione *not quoted here, that Aemilius Paullus took the auspices correctly before Cannae! Note the contrast in the third passage.*

✓   ✓   ✓

1.

I. 25. When, after having reviewed the troops, he [*Flaminius, consul 217 B.C.*] was moving his camp towards Arezzo and leading his legions against Hannibal, his horse suddenly fell with him before the statue of Jupiter Stator, without any apparent cause. But though those who were skilful in divination declared it was an evident sign from the Gods that he should not engage in battle, he paid no attention to it. Afterwards, when it was proposed to consult the auspices by the consecrated chickens, the augur indicated the propriety of deferring the battle. Flaminius asked him what was to be done the next day, if the chickens still refused to feed? He replied that in that case he must still rest quiet. "Fine auspices indeed," replied Flaminius, "if we may only fight when the chickens are hungry, but must do nothing if they are full." And so he commanded the standards to be moved forward, and the army to follow him; on which occasion, the standard-bearer of the first battalion could not extricate his standard from the ground in which it was pitched, and several soldiers who endeavored to assist him were foiled in the attempt. Flaminius, to whom they related this incident, despised the warning, as was usual with him; and in the course of three hours from that time, the whole of his army was routed, and he himself slain [*at Lake Trasimene*].

* From Cicero, *On Divination,* translated by C. D. Yonge (Bohn Classical Library), 1902.

2.

II. 3. [*The speaker is Lucilius (really Cicero, of course*).] Will not the temerity of P. Claudius in the first Punic War affect us? Who, when the poultry were let out of the coop and would not feed, ordered them to be thrown into the water, and joking even upon the Gods, said, with a sneer, "Let them drink, since they will not eat;" which piece of ridicule, being followed by a victory over his fleet, cost him many tears and brought a great calamity on the Roman people. Did not his colleague Junius, in the same war, lose his fleet in a tempest by disregarding the auspices? Claudius therefore was condemned by the people and Junius killed himself. . . . By these instances of calamity we may be assured that Rome owes her grandeur and success to the conduct of those who were tenacious of their religious duties; and if we compare ourselves to our neighbors, we shall find that we are infinitely distinguished above foreign nations by our zeal for religious ceremonies, though in other things we may be only equal to them, and in other respects even inferior to them.

3.

II. 72. Let us reject, therefore, this divination of dreams, as well as all other kinds. For, to speak truly, that superstition has extended itself through all nations, and has oppressed the intellectual energies of almost all men, and has betrayed them into endless imbecilities: as I argued in my treatise On the Nature of the Gods, and as I have especially labored to prove in this dialogue On Divination. For I thought that I should be doing an immense benefit both to myself and to my countrymen if I could entirely eradicate all those superstitious errors.

Nor is there any fear that true religion can be endangered by the demolition of this superstition; for it is the part of a wise man to uphold the religious institutions of our ancestors by the maintenance of their rites and ceremonies. And the beauty of the world and the order of all celestial things compel us to confess that there is an excellent and eternal nature which deserves to be worshipped and admired by all mankind.

4.

II. 24. There is an old saying of Cato, familiar enough
to everybody, that "he wondered that when one soothsayer
met another, he could help laughing."

C. An Impartial Observer of Roman Religion
(Second Century B.C.) *

*Polybius was struck by the scrupulous care with which
the Romans attended to matters of state religion. Certainly it helps to account for the remarkable cohesiveness
of Roman society through the middle Republic; and its
later decline was a cause of the corresponding centripetal
forces in the society. The conservatives in Roman politics
understood this belatedly and attempted to stem the decline. Augustus, of course, gave the closest attention to
matters of traditional religion and morals as well. It will
be noted that Polybius considered the state religion as a
sort of "opium of the masses," to use a Marxian phrase.
However, he probably underestimated the degree to which
upper-class Romans—at least those outside the Scipionic
Circle—actually believed in these rites.*

VI. 56. But the most important difference for the better which the Roman commonwealth appears to me to display is in their religious beliefs. For I conceive that what
in other nations is looked upon as a reproach, I mean a
scrupulous fear of the gods, is the very thing which keeps
the Roman commonwealth together. To such an extraordinary height is this carried among them, both in private
and public business, that nothing could exceed it. Many
people might think this unaccountable; but in my opinion
their object is to use it as a check upon the common
people. If it were possible to form a state wholly of
philosophers, such a custom would perhaps be unneces-
sary. But seeing that every multitude is fickle, and full of
lawless desires, unreasoning anger, and violent passion, the
only resource is to keep them in check by mysterious ter-
rors and scenic effects of this sort.

* From Polybius, *op. cit.*

D.   Morality and the Judgment of God *

This comedy by Plautus was composed during the Second Punic War. The plot, as usual, is Greek, but this section, spoken by a minor god, Arcturus, reflects the Roman, serious view of religion. It is in contrast to some of Plautus' plot material, taken over from the Greeks, which put the gods in hilarious, sometimes even embarrassing positions.

✓   ✓   ✓

(From the Prologue.) "Jove, who is the ruler of gods and men—he disperses us here in various directions among the nations, to observe the actions, manners, piety, and faith of men, just as the means of each avail him. Those who commence villainous suits at law upon false testimony, and those who, in court, upon false oath deny a debt, their names written down, do we return to Jove. Each day does he learn who here is calling for vengeance. Whatever wicked men seek here to gain their cause through perjury, who succeed before the judge in their unjust demands, the same case adjudged does he judge over again, and he fines them in a penalty much greater than the results of the judgment they have gained. The good men written down on other tablets does he keep. And still these wicked persons entertain a notion of theirs, that they are able to appease Jupiter with gifts, with sacrifice; both their labor and their cost they lose. This for this reason, is so, because no petition of the perjured is acceptable to Him. If any person that is supplicating the deities is pious, he will more easily procure pardon for himself than he that is wicked. Therefore I do advise you this, you who are good and who pass your lives in piety and in virtue—still persevere, that one day you may rejoice that so you did."

* From Plautus, *The Fisherman's Rope,* translated by H. T.
   Riley (Bohn Classical Library), 1852.

— Reading No. 9 —

THE CONSTITUTION OF THE REPUBLIC AND ITS DECLINE

A. Optimate View of the Constitution (About 80 B.C.)*

The following passage gives, in a nutshell, the aristocratic view of the Roman constitution; it is not known whether it was a part of some prominent Roman's speech. In any event, it is a quotation of some sort.

✓   ✓   ✓

IV. 35. 47. The Senate's function is to assist the state with counsel; the magistracy's is to execute, by diligent activity, the Senate's will; the people's to choose and support by its votes the best measures and most suitable men.

B. Powers of the Senate (Second Century B.C.) †

Polybius' long residence at Rome and close association with several of the most influential Romans (especially the "Scipionic Circle") qualified him to write accurate descriptions of Roman affairs. Book six of his history gives most valuable information on the constitution of Rome. It is not possible to excerpt here the most significant sections—that would be too lengthy. The following passage illustrates the tremendous economic activity in second-century Rome. It illustrates as well how the growing power of Rome meant an automatic parallel growth in the power of her ruling classes.

✓   ✓   ✓

* Reprinted by permission of the publishers and The Loeb Classical Library from Anonymous, *Ad Herennium,* translated by Harry Caplan, Cambridge, Mass.: Harvard University Press, 1954.
† From Polybius, *op. cit.*

VI. 17. [*The preceding section details how the people, through their Tribunes, could check the power of the Senate.*] In like manner the people on its part is far from being independent of the Senate, and is bound to take its wishes into account both collectively and individually. For contracts, too numerous to count, are given out by the censors in all parts of Italy for the repairs or construction of public buildings; there is also the collection of revenue from many rivers, harbors, gardens, mines, and land—everything, in a word, that comes under the control of the Roman government: and in all these the people at large are engaged; so that there is scarcely a man, so to speak, who is not interested either as a contractor or as being employed in the works. For some purchase the contracts from the censors for themselves; and others go partners with them; while others again go security for these contractors, or actually pledge their property to the treasury for them. Now over all these transactions the Senate has absolute control. It can grant an extension of time; and in case of unforeseen accident can relieve the contractors from a portion of their obligation, or release them from it altogether, if they are absolutely unable to fulfill it. And there are many details in which the Senate can inflict great hardships, or, on the other hand, grant great indulgences to the contractors: for in every case the appeal is to it. But the most important point of all is that the judges are taken from its members in the majority of trials, whether public or private, in which the charges are heavy. Consequently, all citizens are much at its mercy; and being alarmed at the uncertainty as to when they may need its aid, are cautious about resisting or actively opposing its will. And for a similar reason men do not rashly resist the wishes of the Consuls, because one and all may become subject to their absolute authority on a campaign.

C. The Senate's Power Increased Through Custom*

This passage illustrates how the Senate gradually assumed control of one aspect of constitutional procedure

* From M. S. Tanner, *The Commentary of Asconius Pedianus on Cicero's Pro Cornelio* (unpublished M.A. thesis), Chapel Hill, 1942.

—exemption from the laws. In addition it shows how upper-class Romans (even the higher aristocrats) took advantage of their position to profit from moneylending. Cornelius did succeed in getting a law passed which required a quorum of 200 senators for passage of decrees. But he used violence when an opposing tribune vetoed the proposal, and in consequence was later accused of treason (maiestas). *Cicero got him acquitted. Cicero's speech itself is not extant. This is from a commentary of the following century.*

✔   ✔   ✔

Pp. 1f. (Asconius 57). [*C. Cornelius (Piso?) as tribune of the plebs in 67 B.C.*] proposed to the senate that since much money was being delivered to the ambassadors of foreign nations at interest and there were disgraceful and notorious gains from this practice, no one should offer money as a loan to ambassadors of foreign nations. The senate rejected his proposal. . . . Cornelius, offended at the senate by that action, complained of it in a speech before the people. He said that the provinces were being impoverished by loans at interest; that it must be provided that the ambassadors should have resources from which they might pay on the due date.

And he openly proposed a law by which he tried to lessen the authority of the senate to the effect that no one might be exempted from the action of law except through the people [*i.e., the assembly*]. This also had been provided for by law for years; and so in all the decrees of the senate, by which it was decided that anyone be exempted from the laws, it had been customarily added that reference be made to the people on the matter. But gradually they ceased to refer it and at length it had become customary not to add to the decrees of the senate about the carrying of a proposal to the people. And these decrees of the senate were passed through the efforts of just a few.

D. The Will to Power and the Roman Constitution*

Writing of the civil wars of the period A.D. 68-69, Tacitus digresses and gives a summary of the motivations of Roman leaders of the past.

* From Tacitus, *History,* translated by A. J. Church and W. J. Broadribb, London, 1876.

II. 38. That old passion for power which has been ever innate in man increased and broke out as the Empire grew in greatness. In a state of moderate dimensions equality was easily preserved; but when the world had been subdued, when all rival kings and cities had been destroyed, and men had leisure to covet wealth which they might enjoy in security, the early conflicts between the patricians and the people were kindled into flame. At one time the tribunes were factious, at another the consuls had unconstitutional power; it was in the capital and the forum that we first essayed civil wars. Then rose C. Marius, sprung from the very dregs of the populace, and L. Sulla, the most ruthless of the patricians, who perverted into absolute dominion the liberty which had yielded to their arms. After them came Cn. Pompeius, with a character more disguised but no way better. Henceforth men's sole object was supreme power. Legions formed of Roman citizens did not lay down their arms at Pharsalia and Philippi, much less were the armies of Otho and Vitellius [*in A.D. 69*] likely of their own accord to abandon their strife. They were driven into civil war by the same wrath from heaven, the same madness among men, the same incentives to crime.

E.   The Dangers of Extraordinary Commands*

In 67 B.C. the tribune of the plebs, Gabinius, proposed the bill (after passage the Lex Gabinia) *giving to Pompey an extraordinary command of three years' duration against the pirates. One leader of the opposition was Q. Lutatius Catulus, consul in 78 B.C. and long* princeps senatus. *The following account of his remarks, supposedly a speech before the people, is found in Dio, who lived in the late second and early third centuries A.D. The words may of course not be those of Catulus at all, but the writer certainly understood the political views of the* optimates.

* Reprinted by permission of the publisher and The Loeb Classical Library from Dio Cassius, *Roman History*, translated by E. Cary, Cambridge, Mass.: Harvard University Press, 1914.

XXXVI. 31. That I have been exceedingly zealous, Quirites, in behalf of you, the people, you all, no doubt, clearly understand. This being so, it is incumbent upon me to set forth in simple fashion and with frankness what I know to be for the good of the state; and it is only fair for you to listen calmly and then deliberate afterwards. . . . I, for my part, assert first and foremost that it is not proper to entrust to any one man so many positions of command one after another. This has not only been forbidden by the laws, but has also been found by experience to be most perilous. What made Marius what he became was practically nothing else than being entrusted with so many wars in the shortest space of time and being made consul six times in the briefest period; and similarly Sulla became what he was because he held command of the armies so many years in succession, and later was appointed dictator, then consul. For it does not lie in human nature for a person—I speak not alone of the young but of the mature as well—after holding positions of authority for a long period to be willing to abide by ancestral customs. 32. Now I do not say this in any disparagement of Pompey, but because it does not appear ever to have been of advantage to you in any way, and in particular because it is not permitted by the laws. . . .

33. Second, there is the consideration that so long as consuls and praetors and those serving in their places are receiving their offices and commands conformably to the laws it is in no wise fitting, nor yet advantageous, for you to overlook them and introduce some new office. To what end, indeed, do you elect the annual officials, if you are going to make no use of them for such occasions? Surely not that they may stalk about in purple-bordered togas, nor that, clothed with the name alone of office, they may be deprived of its duties. How can you fail to arouse the enmity of these and all the rest who have a purpose to enter public life at all, if you overthrow the ancient offices, and entrust nothing to those elected by law, but assign some strange and hitherto unheard-of command to a private individual? . . .

34. About his, then, I shall say no more. For who does not realize that it is no wise fitting, nor yet advantageous, to entrust affairs to any one man, or for any one man to

be put in control of all the blessings we have, however excellent he may be?

F. The Corrupt Assembly (First Century B.C.)*

Cicero, on the general topic of the two major political factions, argues that the optimate cause was (at least sometimes) really the "popular" cause. In the process he gives some interesting, if perhaps exaggerated information on the working of the assemblies in the mid-first century B.C.

LI. 109. I now come to the Assemblies, whatever their purpose, whether for the election of magistrates or the passing of laws. We often see many laws passed. I say nothing about those which are passed under such conditions that scarcely five in each tribe, and those not from their own tribe, are found to vote. That curse of the State [*Clodius*] says that he passed a law concerning myself, whom he used to call a tyrant and destroyer of liberty. Who is there who admits that he recorded his vote for the proposition against me? But when, in accordance with a decree of the Senate, a law was brought forward at the *comitia centuriata* also about myself, who was there who did not proclaim that he had been present and had voted for my recall? Which cause, then, of the two ought to be considered the popular one? that in which all the respectable men of the State, men of all ages, and all classes, are animated by the same spirit, or that in which frenzied furies flock together as it were to the funeral of the State?

* Reprinted by permission of the publisher and The Loeb Classical Library from Cicero, *Oration for Sestius,* translated by R. Gardner, Cambridge, Mass.: Harvard University Press, 1958.

THE DEVELOPING SYSTEM OF ROMAN LAW

A. A Rhetorician Analyzes Roman Law
(About 80 B.C.)*

This work was long attributed to Cicero. It illustrates the Hellenization of Roman education. It was intended for the rhetorical training of young Romans—with emphasis on oratory in the courts.

Under Stoic influence, especially, Romans had begun to analyze their juridical and legal system. It should be noted that a major source of law, the edicts of the praetors, is not mentioned. Nor is there any mention of the work of jurisconsults like Q. Mucius Scaevola, consul 95 B.C., who must have been a contemporary of the author and whom Cicero much admired for his work in organizing and analyzing of law.

✓ ✓ ✓

II. 13. 19. The departments of which the Law [*ius*] is constituted . . . are the following: Nature [*natura*], Statute [*lex*], Custom [*consuetudo*], Previous Judgments [*iudicata*], Equity [*aequum et bonum*], and Agreement [*pactum*].

To the Law of Nature belong the duties observed because of kinship or family loyalty. In accordance with this kind of Law parents are cherished by their children, and children by their parents.

Statute Law is that kind of Law which is sanctioned by the will of the people; for example, you are to appear before the court when ordered to do so.

Legal Custom is that which, in the absence of any

* From *Ad Herennium, loc. cit.*

statute, is by usage endowed with the force of statute law; for example, the money you have deposited with a banker you may rightly seek from his partner.

It is a Previous Judgment when on the same question a sentence has been passed or a decree interposed. These are often contradictory, according as one judge, praetor, consul, or tribune of the plebs has determined differently from another. . . . For example . . . Gaius Caelius, sitting in judgment, acquitted of the charge of injury [*libel, apparently*] the man who had by name attacked the poet Lucilius on the stage, while Publius Mucius condemned the man who had specifically named the poet Lucius Accius. . . .

The Law rests on Equity when it seems to agree with truth and the general welfare; for example, a man who is more than sixty years old, and pleads illness, shall substitute an attorney for himself. . . .

It is Law founded on Agreement if the parties have made some contract between themselves—if there is some covenant between parties. . . .

B. Inalienable Rights in Roman Law (First Century B.C.)*

Cicero argues in favor of a number of basic rights which were not conferred by (statute) law and which could not be removed by law.

✦   ✦   ✦

XXIX. The law was established by our ancestors, who were not fictitiously and pretendedly attached to the people, but were so in truth and wisdom, in such a manner that no Roman citizen could be deprived of his liberty against his consent. Moreover, if the decemvirs [*450 B.C.*] had given an unjust decision to the prejudice of any one's liberty, they established a law that any one who chose might, on this subject alone, make a motion affecting a formal decision already pronounced. But no one will ever lose his status as a citizen against his will by any vote of the people.

XXX. The Roman citizens who left Rome and went to the Latin colonies could not be made Latins, unless they

* From Cicero, *Oration on His Own House,* loc. cit.

themselves promoted such a change, and gave in their
names themselves. Those men who had been condemned
on a capital charge, did not lose their rights as citizens of
this city before they were received as citizens of that other
city to which they had gone for the sake of changing
their abode. Our ancestors took care that they should do
so, not by taking away their rights of citizenship, but only
their house, and by interdicting them from fire and water
within the city. The Roman people on the motion of Lucius Sulla, the dictator, in the comitia centuriata, took
away the rights of citizenship from the municipal towns,
and at the same time took away their lands. The decree
about the lands was ratified, for that the people had power
to pass; but their decree concerning the rights of citizenship did not last even as long as the disturbances of the
time of Sulla. Shall we then say that Lucius Sulla, victorious as he was, after he had been restored to the republic, could not in the comitia centuriata take away the
rights of citizenship from the people of Volaterra, even
though they were in arms at the time;—and the Volater-
rans to this day enjoy the rights of citizenship with ourselves. . . .

Our ancestors, then, . . . established those principles
which neither the power of time, nor the authority of
magistrates, not the decisions of judges, nor the sovereign
power of the whole people of Rome, which in all other
affairs is most absolute, can undermine.

— Reading No. 11 —

FIRST INTERVENTION EAST OF THE ADRIATIC (ABOUT 230 B.C.)*

The historian tells of the piracy which led to the first Roman intervention in the Adriatic—significant for later relations with King Philip V of Macedonia. Note also the developed concept of a "law of nations" (although the specific term is here added by the translator).

✓   ✓   ✓

II. 8. To return to the Illyrians. From time immemorial they had oppressed and pillaged vessels sailing from Italy: and now while their fleet was engaged at Phoenice a considerable number of them, separating from the main body, committed acts of piracy on a number of Italian merchants; some they merely plundered, others they murdered, and a great many they carried off alive into captivity. Now, though complaints against the Illyrians had reached the Roman government in times past, they had always been neglected; but now when more and more persons approached the Senate on this subject, they appointed two ambassadors, Gaius and Lucius Coruncanius, to go to Illyricum and investigate the matter. But on the arrival of her galleys from Epirus, the enormous quantity and beauty of the spoils which they brought home (for Phoenice was by far the wealthiest city in Epirus at that time), so fired the imagination of Queen Teuta, that she was doubly eager to carry on the predatory warfare on the coasts of Greece.

At the moment, however, she was stopped by the rebellion at home; but it had not taken her long to put down the revolt in Illyria, and she was engaged in besieging Issa, the last town which held out, when just at that very

* From Polybius, *op. cit.*

time the Roman ambassadors arrived. A time was fixed for their audience, and they proceeded to discuss the injuries which their citizens had sustained. Throughout the interview, however, Teuta listened with an insolent and disdainful air; and when they had finished their speech, she replied that she would endeavor to take care that no injury should be inflicted on Roman citizens by Illyrian officials; but that it was not the custom for the sovereigns of Illyria to hinder private persons from taking booty at sea.

Angered by these words, the younger of the two ambassadors used a plainness of speech which, though thoroughly to the point, was rather ill-timed. "The Romans," he said, "O Teuta, have a most excellent custom of using the State for the punishment of private wrongs and the redress of private grievances: and we will endeavor, God willing, before long to compel you to improve the relations between the sovereign and the subject in Illyria." The queen received this plain speaking with womanish passion and unreasoning anger. So enraged was she at the speech that, in despite of the conventions universally observed among mankind, she despatched some men after the ambassadors, as they were sailing home, to kill the one who had used this plainness. Upon this being reported at Rome the people were highly incensed at the queen's violation of the law of nations, and at once set about preparations for war, enrolling legions and collecting a fleet.

ROMAN MORAL FIBER AND ITS DECLINE

A. A Roman of the Old School (Second Century B.C.)*

L. Aemilius Paullus and his son, P. Cornelius Scipio Aemilianus, had great reputations for honesty in matters of money. The following passage illustrates this well enough. This information derives from Polybius XXXI, 22 ff., but is here taken from Diodorus for the interesting contrast made in the last sentences. These remarks were made in the late first century B.C.

✓   ✓   ✓

XXXI. 26. This same Aemilius in departing this life left behind him a reputation for character equal to that which he had enjoyed while living. For though he had brought to Rome, from Spain, more gold than any of his contemporaries, had had in his possession the fabulous treasures of Macedonia, and had had unlimited powers in the said cases, he so completely abstained from appropriating any of this money that after his death his sons, whom he had given in adoption, on receiving their inheritance were unable to pay off from the whole of his personal property the dowry of his widow, except by selling some of the real property as well. Hence it seemed to many that in freedom from avarice he had outdone even those who were the marvel of Greece in this respect, Aristeides and Epaminondas. For they had refused gifts whenever the offer was made in the interest of the donors, but he, with

* Reprinted by permission of the publisher and The Loeb Classical Library from Diodorus of Sicily, *Universal History,* translated by F. R. Walton, Cambridge, Mass.: Harvard University Press, 1957.

full power to take as much as he wanted, had coveted nothing. Now if this statement seems incredible to some, they should take into account the fact that we cannot properly judge the freedom of the ancients from avarice by the dishonest greed of present-day Romans. For in our lifetime this people has, it appears, acquired a strong tendency to want more and more.

B.   Peace Brings Relaxation of Morals*

Sallust, a moralistic and somewhat cynical historian of the first century B.C., dated Roman social and moral decline from the time of final victory over the Carthaginians, 146 B.C. One should allow for exaggeration.

⟶   ⟶   ⟶

(A Fragment.) When, after the terror of the Carthaginians was removed, the people were at liberty to resume their dissensions, innumerable disturbances, seditions, and subsequent civil wars, arose, while a few powerful individuals, whose interest most of the other nobles had submitted to promote, sought, under the specious pretext of supporting the senate or the plebians, to secure power for themselves; and men were esteemed, or despised by them, not as they deserved well or ill of the republic (for all were equally corrupt), but whoever grew eminently wealthy, and better able to encroach on others, was styled, if he supported the present state of affairs, an excellent citizen. From this period, the manners of our forefathers degenerated, not, as before, gradually, but with precipitation, like that of a torrent; and the youth became so depraved with luxury and avarice, that they might be thought, with justice, to have been born powerless either to preserve their own property, or to suffer others to preserve theirs.

C.   A Bad Provincial Governor, 73-71 B.C.†

Cicero's prosecution of Verres in 70 B.C. exposed the venality of at least some of Rome's provincial governors.

* From Sallust, *History* (fragment), translated by J. S. Watson, New York, 1855.
† From Cicero, *Against Verres,* translated by C. D. Yonge (Bohn Classical Library), 1887.

*Verres had served as governor (propraetor) of Sicily.
Cicero's extant speeches were not all actually delivered
before the court. There was need for haste or the case
might have been put off indefinitely. These orations provide us with much information regarding provincial government in general and venal practices in particular. Some
allowance must be made for the bias of a prosecutor.
Verres, unable to meet the charges, went into exile. Since
one of Verres' lawyers was Q. Hortensius, hitherto the
leading advocate in Rome, Cicero now displaced him as
the best orator of the city. The first section below was a
kind of introductory indictment.*

I. 4. While this man [*Verres*] was praetor the Sicilians
enjoyed neither their own laws nor the decrees of our
senate nor the common rights of every nation. Every one
in Sicily has only so much left as either escaped the
notice or was disregarded by the satiety of the most avari-
cious and licentious man.

5. No legal decision for three years was given on any
other ground but his will; no property was so secure to
any man, even if it had descended to him from his father
and grandfather, but he was deprived of it at his command; enormous sums of money were exacted from the
property of the cultivators of the soil by a new and
nefarious system. The most faithful of the allies were
classed in the number of enemies. Roman citizens were
tortured and put to death like slaves; the greatest criminals
were acquitted in the courts of justice through bribery;
the most upright and honorable men, being prosecuted
while absent, were condemned and banished without being
heard in their own defense; the most fortified harbors, the
greatest and strongest cities, were laid open to pirates and
robbers; the sailors and soldiers of the Sicilians, our own
allies and friends, died of hunger; the best built fleets on
the most important stations were lost and destroyed, to
the great disgrace of the Roman people. This same man
while praetor plundered and stripped those most ancient
monuments, some erected by wealthy monarchs and intended by them as ornaments for their cities; some, too,
the work of our own generals, which they either gave or
restored as conquerors to the different states in Sicily.

And he did this not only in the case of public statues and ornaments, but he also plundered all the temples consecrated in the deepest religious feelings of the people. He did not leave, in short, one god to the Sicilians which appeared to him to be made in a tolerably workmanlike manner, and with any of the skill of the ancients.

*   *   *

V. 14. I will relate to you this fact, O judges, most truly. I recollect that Pamphilus of Lilybaeum, a connexion of mine by ties of hospitality, and a personal friend of mine, a man of the highest birth, told me that when that man had taken from him by his absolute power an ewer made by the hands of Boethus, of exquisite workmanship and great weight, he went home very sad in truth, and greatly agitated, because a vessel of that sort, which had been left to him by his father and his forefathers and which he was accustomed to use on days of festival and on the arrival of ancient friends, had been taken from him. While I was sitting at home, said he, in great indignation, up comes one of the slaves of Venus; he orders me immediately to bring to the praetor some embossed goblets. I was greatly vexed, said he; I had two; I order them both to be taken out of the closet lest any worse thing should happen, and to be brought after me to the praetor's house. When I got there the praetor was asleep; the Cibyratic brothers were walking about, and when they saw me, they said, Pamphilus, where are the cups? I show them with great grief;—they praise them. I begin to complain that I shall have nothing left of any value at all, if my cups too were taken away. Then they, when they see me vexed, say, What are you willing to give us to prevent these from being taken from you? To make my story short I said that I would give six hundred sesterces. Then they began to say to the praetor that they had thought from what they had heard, that Pamphilus's cups were of some value, but that they were miserable things, quite unworthy of Verres's having them among his plate. He said he thought so too. So Pamphilus saved his exquisite goblets.

D. An Attack on Senator-Jurors, 70 B.C.*

The Senator-jurors after Sulla (as before Gaius Grac-
chus) sometimes dispensed more mercy than justice to
members of the governing class. Cicero's remarks here in
his prosecution of Verres may have helped sway public
opinion in favor of reform.

✓   ✓   ✓

I. 1. That which was above all things to be desired,
O judges, and which above all things was calculated to
have the greatest influence towards allaying the unpopu-
larity of your order, and putting an end to the discredit
into which your judicial decisions have fallen, appears to
have been thrown in your way, and given to you not by
any human contrivance, but almost by the interposition
of the gods, at a most important crisis of the republic.
For an opinion has now become established, pernicious to
us, and pernicious to the republic, which has been the
common talk of every one, not only at Rome, but among
foreign nations also—that in the courts of law as they
exist at present, no wealthy man, however guilty he may
be, can possibly be convicted. . . . You have an opportunity of retrieving the lost credit of your judicial proceedings, of regaining your credit with the Roman people,
and of giving satisfaction to foreign nations; a man, the
embezzler of the public funds, the petty tyrant of Asia
and Pamphylia, the robber who deprived the city of its
rights, the disgrace and ruin of the province of Sicily.
And if you come to a decision about this man with severity
and a due regard to your oaths, that authority which
ought to remain in you will cling to you still; but if that
man's vast riches shall break down the sanctity and honesty of the courts of justice, at least I shall achieve this,
that it shall be plain that it was rather honest judgment
that was wanting to the republic, than a criminal to the
judges, or an accuser to the criminal.

* *Ibid.*

POLITICAL FACTIONS OF THE LATE REPUBLIC: POPULARIS VS. OPTIMATE

A. Factionalism: The Problem*

This little passage may perform a very important service if by it the student is reminded that popularis *leaders were usually senators and were usually supported by a strong segment of the senate. The factionalism of the late Republic should not be thought of as a struggle between democracy and oligarchy. The chief difference between the factions was one of method.*

✓　　　✓　　　✓

I. 15. 31. How can there be two senates in one Commonwealth, and, as it were, two distinct peoples? For, as you see, the death of Tiberius Gracchus and the whole system of his tribuneship, has divided one people into two parties. But the slanderers and the enemies of Scipio, encouraged by P. Crassus and Appius Claudius, maintained, after the death of these two chiefs, a division of nearly half the senate, under the influence of Metellus and Mucius. Nor would they permit the man [*Scipio Aemilianus*] who alone could have been of service, to help us out of our difficulties during the movement of the Latins and allies towards rebellion, violating all our treaties in the presence of factious triumvirs, and creating every day some fresh intrigue, to the disturbance of the worthier and wealthier citizens.

* From Cicero, *On the Republic,* adapted from translation by C. D. Yonge (Bohn Classical Library), 1902.

B. Cicero Explains Who Are "Optimates" *

*This speech was given in February, 56 B.C., in defense
of a man who as tribune the preceding year had worked
for Cicero's recall from exile. It came at a time when it
appeared the so-called first triumvirate might break up.
Cicero, much encouraged, tried to advance, once more,
what was really his* concordia ordinum. *In the process
he defines—from a partisan point of view, to be sure—
the two main political groups of the state: the* populares
and the optimates, *essentially untranslatable terms.*

✓   ✓   ✓

XLIV. 96. You made a point of asking me especially
what was the meaning of our "Breed of Aristocrats," to
use your own term. You ask about a matter, which is
most proper for the young to learn, while it is not difficult for me to offer some instruction; and I will say a
few words about it, gentlemen, nor, I think, will what I
say be irrelevant, either to the advantage of those who
hear me, or to the discharge of your duties, or to the case
itself of Publius Sestius.

XLV. There have always been two classes of men in
this State who have sought to engage in public affairs and
to distinguish themselves in them. Of these two classes,
one aimed at being, by repute and in reality, "Friends of
the People," [*populares*] the other "Aristocrats" [*optimates*]. Those who wished everything they did and said
to be agreeable to the masses were reckoned as "Friends
of the People," but those who acted so as to win by their
policy the approval of all the best [*optimi*] citizens were
reckoned as "Aristocrats." "Who then are these 'Best
Citizens' of yours?" In number, if you ask me, they are
infinite: for otherwise we could not exist. They include
those who direct the policy of the State, with those who
follow their lead. They include those very large classes to
whom the Senate is open; they include Romans living in
municipal towns and in country districts; they include
men of business; freemen also are among the "Aristo-

* Reprinted by permission of the publisher and The Loeb
  Classical Library from Cicero, *Oration for Sestius,* translated by R. Gardner, Cambridge, Mass.: Harvard University Press, 1958.

crats." In its numbers, I repeat, this class is spread far
and wide and is variously composed. But, to prevent mis-
understanding, the whole class can be summed up and
defined in a few words. All are "Aristocrats" who are
neither criminal nor vicious in disposition, nor mad revo-
lutionaries, nor embarrassed by home troubles. It follows,
then, that those who are upright, sound in mind, and easy
in circumstances are those whom you have called a
"Breed." Those who serve the wishes, the interests and
principles of these men in the government of the State
are called the supporters of the "Aristocrats" and are
themselves reckoned as the most influential of the "Aristocrats," the most eminent citizens, and the leaders of
the State. What then is the mark set before those who
guide the helm of state, upon which they ought to keep
their eyes and towards which they ought to direct their
course? It is that which is far the best and most desirable
for all who are sound and good and prosperous; it is
"Peace with Honor [*cum dignitate otium*]." Those who
desire this are all reckoned as "Aristocrats," those who
achieve it as the foremost men and the saviors of the
State. For just as it is unfitting for men to be so carried
away by the honor of public office that they are indifferent to peace, so too it is unfitting for them to welcome a
peace which is inconsistent with honor.

XLVI. Now this "Peace with Honor" has the following
foundations, the following elements, which our leaders
ought to protect and defend even at the risk of life itself:
religious observances, the auspices, the powers of the
magistrates, the authority of the Senate, the laws, ancestral custom [*mos maiorum*], criminal and civil jurisdiction,
credit [*fides*], our provinces, our allies, the prestige of our
government, the army, the treasury.

C. A Popular Tribune Excoriates the Ruling Class, 73 B.C.*

*This speech of C. Licinius Macer illustrates the sort of
agitation which, when combined with war, depression,
and the ambition of individuals, led to the dissolution of
Sulla's constitution. The words are probably those of
Sallust rather than Macer. However, Sallust was something of a* popularis, *and it is likely that he recorded*

* From Sallust, *History, loc. cit.*

genuine sentiments and attitudes. Note that a chief griev-
ance was a lack of "liberty" which (see last sentence)
was practically defined as sharing equitably in the spoils
of empire.

✓   ✓   ✓

(A Fragment.) [*The magistrates have*] submitted themselves to the rule of a faction, who, on the pretense of
conducting a war, have assumed the control of the treasury and the army, of kingdoms and provinces, and have
built, as it were, out of the spoils taken from you, a
stronghold for your oppression; while you, like a tame
herd, yield yourselves, notwithstanding the greatness of
your numbers, to be possessed and fleeced by a few, and
robbed of all that your ancestors left you except the power
of electing magistrates, who were once your defenders
and are now your tyrants. . . .

You yourselves, my fellow citizens, by executing these
lordly commands of the consuls and decrees of the senators, give them your sanction and authority, and increase
and strengthen the despotism exercised over you. Not, I
say, that I would persuade you to revenge your injuries,
but rather to remain at rest; nor do I demand restitution
of your rights from a love of discord, as they falsely
charge upon me, but from a desire to see an end of discord; and if they obstinately refuse you justice, I do not
recommend armed violence or a secession, but only that
you should forbear to shed your blood in their behalf. Let
them hold and exercise their offices in their own way; let
them obtain triumphs; let them pursue Mithradates as
well as Sertorius and the remnant of the exiles, with their
trains of statues and images [*of their noble ancestors (see
Reading No. 6B)*]; but let danger and toil be far from
you, who have no share in the advantage of them; unless
indeed your services have been repaid by the late law,
so suddenly passed, for the distribution of grain; . . .
they have estimated the liberty of each individual at the
price of ten gallons [*five modii*] of grain. . . .

D.   An Optimate Excoriates Popular Tribunes
(About 45 B.C.)*

The attack is mounted chiefly (in dialogue) by Quintus Cicero with an unenthusiastic defense by Marcus (the real author).

✓   ✓   ✓

III. 8. QUINTUS: I beg your pardon, my brother, but I particularly wish to know your opinion of this power of the tribunes. To me it appears extremely mischievous, at once the child and parent of endless seditions. If we look back to the origin of the tribunate, we find that it originally sprang up at a time of civil disturbances, when all the chief places of the city were either occupied or besieged. After this, being soon stifled, as one of those monstrous abortions which, by a law of the Twelve Tables, are not suffered to live, it again recovered its existence, only to become baser and viler than ever.

9. For what kind of atrocity did it leave undone? Its first act was a piece of villainy well worthy of its impious character, namely, the abrogation of the honors of the senate and patricians. It reduced the highest ranks to an equality with the meanest, agitating and confounding all things. When it had thus insulted and violated the gravity of our nobles, it was still as insane and insensate as before. Not to mention a Flaminius and others, which you may call antiquated instances, what laws or rights did the tribune Tiberius Gracchus leave to the best and worthiest citizens? And five years before, did not the tribune Caius Curiatus, the basest and foulest of mortals, cast into prison the consuls Decimus Brutus and Publius Scipio, men of the greatest eminence?—a thing which was wholly unprecedented. And did not C. Gracchus endeavor to overturn and revolutionize our whole commonwealth, by throwing darts and daggers into the forum, as he himself avowed, in order to excite the citizens to mutual slaughter, as if they were so many gladiators? Why need I speak of the crimes of Saturninus and others, whose violences the commonwealth could scarcely repel without civil war? But why should we mention these antique

* From Cicero, *On the Laws,* translated by C. D. Yonge (Bohn Classical Library), 1902.

instances, belonging to other ages, when so many have occurred within our own memory? Who was ever so audacious and so inimical to us, as to nourish a thought of destroying our state, without he had first sharpened some sword or a tribune against us? And when infamous and profligate men could not find, not only in any house, but not even in any nation, any such instrument, they endeavored to create disturbances among the people in the darkest places of the republic.

And what does us infinite honor, and secures us immortal renown, is the fact, that no tribune could be engaged to appear against us by any bribe whatever, except that one who could not legally be a tribune at all [*Clodius, 58 B.C.*], who used the tribunate as a cloak of villainy. As for this monster, what crimes did he not perpetrate— crimes which, without reason or plausible hope, he committed with the fury of some savage beast, maddened with the violence of the brutal mob. I therefore highly approve of the conduct of Sulla in this particular, inasmuch as by his law he rendered the tribunes of the people comparatively impotent for mischief, though he left them the power of giving assistance. As for our friend Pompey, in all other respect I extoll him with the amplest and warmest praises,—I say nothing of his views relating to the power of the tribunes; for here I cannot praise him, and yet I would not censure him.

10. MARCUS: You have very clearly unfolded, my Quintus, the defects and abuses of the tribunate; but it is unfair, with respect to any matter which one is impeaching, to state all its faults, dwell upon all its evils, and omit its merits. For in this way you might make out the consulate itself to be a very culpable and objectional institution, if you were to reckon up all the sins of some consuls, whom I am willing to pass in silence. For even in this power, I confess there are some stains of evil; but we can never obtain the good which we aimed at in its establishment without those particles of evil. That the authority of the tribunes of the people is too great, none will deny; but the power of the people themselves is much more cruel, and much more violent; and by having a leader, therefore, such as a tribune, they often behave more temperately than if they had no one at all. For a leader remembers that he is advancing at his own risk,

whereas the violence of the people has no consideration
for its own danger; sometimes it is suddenly excited, and
again it is often tranquillized. For what body of men can
be so insane, that not one in ten of its members preserves
his senses?

— Reading No. 14 —

REACTION TO ROMAN
INTERVENTION IN THE EAST

**A. Early Philhellenic Liberalism Evokes Enthusiastic
Response, 196 B.C.***

*After the victory over Philip V of Macedonia the Ro-
mans had to decide what their policy would be toward
Greece in general. They could play the role that Macedonia had played, holding on to the "fetters of Greece"
—Corinth, Chalcis, and Demetrias; they could withdraw
entirely; or they could depend on a policy of "friendship"
—in Roman custom almost equivalent to alliance—which
would tend to make clients of the Greek states. The latter
course was determined upon. It is to be feared the Greeks
did not fully understand the Roman position. In any case
the Roman decision not to dominate Greece openly was
at first a popular one, as this reading indicates.*

1   1   1

X. It was now the time of the celebration of the
Isthmian games [*near Corinth*]; and the seats around the
racecourse were crowded with an unusual multitude of
spectators; Greece, after long wars, having regained not
only peace, but hopes of liberty, and being able once more
to keep holiday in safety. A trumpet sounded to com-

* From Plutarch, *Flamininus,* translated by J. Dryden and
others, rev. A. H. Clough, London, 1864.

mand silence; and the crier, stepped forth amidst the spectators, made proclamation, that the Roman senate and Titus Quinctius, the proconsular general, having vanquished King Philip and the Macedonians, restored the Corinthians, Locrians, Phocians, Euboeans, Achaeans of Phthiotis, Magnetians, Thessalians, and Perrhaebians to their own lands, laws, and liberties; remitting all impositions upon them, and withdrawing all garrisons from their cities. At first, many heard not at all and others not distinctly, what was said; but there was a confused and uncertain stir among the assembled people, some wondering, some asking, some calling out to have it proclaimed again. A shout of joy followed it, so loud that it was heard as far as the sea. The whole assembly rose and stood up; there was no further thought of the entertainment: all were only eager to leap up and salute and address their thanks to the deliverer and champion of Greece.

What we often hear alleged, in proof of the force of human voices, was actually verified upon this occasion. Crows that were accidentally flying over the course fell down dead into it. This disruption of the air must be the cause of it; for the voices being numerous, and the acclamation violent, the air breaks with it and can no longer give support to the birds, but lets them tumble, like one that should attempt to walk upon a vacuum; unless we should rather imagine them to fall and die, shot with the noise as a dart. It is possible, too, that there may be a circular agitation of the air, which, like marine whirlpools, may have a violent direction of this sort given to it from the excess of its fluctuation.

B. A Roman Embassy to the East, 169-168 B.C.*

Rome's tendency to demand close cooperation from "friends" as if they were allies is indicated in the first passage. A correlative tendency of her ambassadors to assume great authority is indicated in the second passage. The incident in the latter passage is hardly typical.

✓ ✓ ✓

XXXIII. 3. Aulus [*Hostilius*] being . . . Proconsul . . . sent Gaius Popilius and Gnaeus Octavius to visit

* From Polybius, *op. cit.*

certain places in Greece. They came first to Thebes, where, after speaking in complimentary terms of the Thebans, they exhorted them to maintain their good disposition towards Rome. They then went a round of the cities in the Peloponnese, and endeavored to convince the people of the clemency and humanity of the Senate by producing the decree which I recently mentioned [*forbidding Roman commanders to requisition supplies unless approved by the Senate*]. At the same time they made it clearly understood that the Senate was aware who in the several states were hanging back and trying to evade their obligations, and who were forward and zealous; and they let it be seen that they were as much displeased with those who thus hung back as with those who openly took the opposite side [*i.e., of Macedonia*]. This brought hesitation and doubt to the minds of the people at large, as to how to frame their words and actions so as to exactly suit the necessities of the times.

*   *   *

[*The following year, the ambassadors went on to Egypt.*] XXIX. 27. When Antiochus [*IV*] had advanced to attack Ptolemy in order to possess himself of Pelusium, he was met by the Roman commander Gaius Popilius Laenus. Upon the king greeting him from some distance, and holding out his right hand to him, Popilius answered by holding out the tablets which contained the decree of the Senate, and bade Antiochus read that first: not thinking it right, I suppose, to give the usual sign of friendship until he knew the mind of the recipient, whether he were to be regarded as a friend or foe. On the king, after reading the despatch, saying that he desired to consult with his friends on the situation, Popilius did a thing which was looked upon as exceedingly overbearing and insolent. Happening to have a vine stick in his hand, he drew a circle round Antiochus with it, and ordered him to give his answer to the letter before he stepped out of that circumference. The king was taken aback by this haughty proceeding. After a brief interval of embarrassed silence, he replied that he would do whatever the Romans demanded. Then Popilius and his colleagues shook him by the hand, and one and all greeted him with warmth. The contents of the despatch was an order to put an end to the war with Ptolemy at once. Accordingly a stated number of days was allowed him, within which he withdrew his army into Syria, in high dudgeon, indeed, and groaning in spirit, but yielding to the necessities of the time.

C. Purported Speech of Mithradates; Hopes for Success (About 89 B.C.)*

Pompeius Trogus, son of a minor official under Caesar, criticized Livy and Sallust for including speeches which illustrated chiefly their own eloquence. Presumably he had reason to think these words of Mithradates fairly exact. Note especially the last sentence.

✓   ✓   ✓

XXXVIII. 4. He had heard that the Romans had been overthrown in three battles by Pyrrhus, when he had with him not more than five thousand Macedonians; he had heard that Hannibal continued victorious in Italy for sixteen years, and that it was not the strength of the Romans, but the violence of his own countrymen's envy and jealousy that prevented him from taking the city of Rome itself; he had heard that the people of Transalpine Gaul had invaded Italy, and founded many great cities in it, and that the same Gauls had possessed themselves of a larger territory there than in Asia, though Asia was considered by no means a warlike country; he had been informed that Rome was not only taken but conquered by the Gauls, the top of one hill only being left in possession of the inhabitants, and that the enemy was not made to retire by the sword, but by gold. . . . Not to dwell on past instances, [*he declared that*] all Italy at the present time was in arms in the Marsian [*Social*] war, demanding, not liberty, but a participation in the government and the rights of citizenship. Nor was the city more grievously harassed by war from its neighbors in Italy than by intestine broils among its leading men; and that a civil war, indeed, was much more dangerous to it than an Italian one.

*   *   *

* From Justin, *Epitome of Pompeius Trogus' Philippic Histories,* translated by J. S. Watson (Bohn Classical Library), 1886.

XXXVIII. 6. "No king's services were thought more important by them than those of Masinissa, king of Numidia; to him it was ascribed that Hannibal was conquered; to him, that Syphax was made prisoner; to him, that Carthage was destroyed; he was ranked with the two [*Scipio*] Africani as a third savior of the city; yet a war had lately been carried on with his grandson [*Jugurtha*] in Africa so implacably that they would not save the vanquished prince, for the sake of his grandfather's memory, from being cast into gaol, and led in triumph as a public spectacle. That they had made it a law to themselves to hate all kings, because they themselves had had such kings at whose names they might well blush . . . their founders, according to their report, were suckled by the teats of a wolf, so the whole race had the disposition of wolves, being insatiable of blood and tyranny, and eager and hungry after riches.

XXXVIII. 7. "Asia so eagerly expected him that it even invited him in words, so much had the rapacity of the proconsuls, the sales of the tax-gatherers, and the disgraceful mode of conducting law-suits, possessed the people with a hatred of the Romans."

D. Athenians Persuaded to Join Mithradates (About 88 B.C.)*

The bitter feeling of many Greeks toward Roman domination is well illustrated in this purported speech of one Aristion. Sent as an ambassador of Mithradates, he persuaded Athenians to ally themselves with Mithradates. Aristion himself was made chief general and soon assumed the sole authority of a tyrant.

This quotation comes from the Greek Alexandrian Athenaeus, who lived and wrote at Rome in the early third century A.D. However, it is a direct quotation from Posidonius of Rhodes. The latter was an eminent scholar and Stoic teacher of the first century B.C. One of his pupils and friends was Cicero. Posidonius' history was a continuation of Polybius. The speech cannot, of course, be considered the exact words of the speaker, but Posi-

---

* From Athenaeus, *Doctors at Dinner,* translated by C. D. Yonge (Bohn Classical Library), 1854.

donius understood well enough the contemporary Greek spirit.

✔   ✔   ✔

V. 51. O men of Athens . . . I tell you . . . of things which have never been hoped for nor even imagined. . . . The King Mithradates is master of Bithynia, and of Upper Cappadocia; and he is master of the whole of Asia, without any break, as far as Pamphylia and Cilicia: and the kings of the Armenians and Persians are only his guards; and he is lord of all the nations which dwell around the Palus Maeotis and the whole of Pontus, so that his dominions are upwards of thirty thousand furlongs in circumference. And the Roman commander in Pamphylia, Quintus Oppius, has been surrendered to him, and is following him as a prisoner, but Manius Aquillius, a man of consular rank who has celebrated a triumph for his victory over the Sicilians, is fastened by a long chain to Bastarna, a man of gigantic stature, and is dragged by him on foot at the tail of his horse. . . .

And every city honoring him [*Mithradates*] with more than human honors, calls the king a god; and oracles everywhere promise him the dominion over the whole world, on which account he is now sending large armies against Thrace and Macedonia, and every part of Europe is coming over bodily to his side. For ambassadors are coming to him, not only from the Italian tribes, but also from the Carthaginians, begging him to enter into alliance with them for the destruction of the Romans. . . .

What then do I advise?—Not to bear this state of anarchy any longer, which the Roman senate makes continue, while it is deciding what constitution you are to enjoy for the future. And do not let us be indifferent to our temples being closed, to our gymnasia being left in the dirt, to our theatre being always empty, and our courts of justice mute, and the Pnyx, consecrated by the oracles of the gods, being taken from the people. Let us not, O Athenians, be indifferent to the sacred voice of Bacchus being reduced to silence, to the holy temple of Castor and Pollux being closed, and to the schools of the philosophers being silenced as they are.

E. The Dilemma of a Roman Provincial Governor, 60 B.C.*

This is an extract from a letter from Marcus Cicero to his brother Quintus, written when the latter was governor of the province of Asia (approximately the former Kingdom of Pergamum). It shows how difficult it was to govern in the interests of the people and also in the interests of Rome. The publicans were rich equestrian or middle-class Romans who bid for the privilege of collecting taxes in the province. Conciliating this group was an essential part of Cicero's concordia ordinum. The tax contractors at this time were losing money and were trying to get the Senate to revise the contracts. Cato opposed this; Crassus favored it; one of the chief benefits of the "first triumvirate" for him was a reduction in the contracts.

a   a   a

I. 1. It seems to require a superhuman virtue . . . to give satisfaction to the farmers of the public revenue (*publicani*), especially when the taxes have been disadvantageously contracted for, and at the same time not to suffer our allies to be ruined.

But, in the first place, as to the Greeks, the hardship which they most bitterly complain of, that of their being taxed, is, in my opinion, no great hardship, because by their own constitutions, apart from the government of the Roman people, they were in the same condition with their own consent. As to the name of a farmer of the revenue, the Greeks ought not to hold it in such contempt, because, without their assistance, they could not have paid the tax indiscriminately imposed upon them by Sulla.

Now that the Greeks are fully as severe as our farmers are, in the collection of the public revenue, may be concluded from this, that the Caunians some time ago, who inhabit the islands that were annexed by Sulla to the division of Rhodes, petitioned the senate that they might pay their taxes to us rather than to the Rhodians. They therefore who always have been taxed, ought not to hold

* From Cicero, *Letters to His Brother Quintus*, translated by C. R. Edmonds (Harper's Classical Library), 1855.

the name of a tax-gatherer with horror, nor ought they to despise him, without whom they can not pay their taxes; nor ought they who have petitioned for him to reject him. The Asiatics ought at the same time to reflect, that were they not under our government, no calamity of foreign war and domestic discussion would ever have been absent from them. And since this government can not be supported without taxes, they ought cheerfully to purchase for themselves, with some part of their incomes, an uninterrupted peace and tranquillity. When once they come to endure with patience the profession and name of a farmer of the revenue, your prudent measures and conduct will be able to make other annoyances seem lighter to them. They will come, not to reflect so much in making their compositions upon the Censorian Law, but rather upon the advantage of settling the business, and upon their freedom from molestation. You can likewise continue what you have always so admirably done, to put them in mind how much dignity there is in the office of a farmer of the revenue, and how much we owe to that order. So that, apart from force and the influence of authority, and of the fasces, you will bring the publicans into favor and credit with the Greeks. You may even entreat those whom you have so highly obliged, and who owe their all to you, that by their compliance they will suffer us to cherish and continue those intimate connections that subsist between us and the farmers of the revenue.

— Reading No. 15 —

SOME PERSONAL GLIMPSES

A. The Elder Scipio Africanus*

No matter what their intentions, the Scipios in some ways were the forerunners of the revolutionary leaders of the late Republic. Even in their own times they were attacked by Cato and others for their tendency to use their status as heroes to run roughshod over the ordinary constitutional procedures. The following passage from Diodorus illustrates the anti-Scipionic view.

✓   ✓   ✓

XXIX. 21. Because of his great achievements Scipio wielded more influence than seemed compatible with the dignity of the state. Once, for example, being charged with an offence punishable by a painful death, he said only, when it was his turn to speak, that it ill behooved Romans to cast a vote against the man to whom his very accusers owed their enjoyment of the right to speak freely. At these words the whole populace, shamed by the force of his remark, left the meeting at once, and his accuser, deserted and alone, returned home discredited. On another occasion, at a meeting of the senate, when funds were needed and the quaestor refused to open the treasury, Scipio took over the keys to do it himself, saying that it was thanks to him that the quaestors were in fact able to lock it. On still another occasion, when someone in the senate demanded from him an accounting of the monies he had received to maintain his troops, he acknowledged that he had the account but refused to render it, on the

* Reprinted by permission of the publisher and The Loeb Classical Library from Diodorus of Sicily, *Universal History,* translated by F. R. Walton, Cambridge, Mass.: Harvard University Press, 1957.

ground that he ought not to be subjected to scrutiny on the same basis as others. When his accuser pressed the demand, he sent to his brother, had the book brought into the senate chamber, and after tearing it to bits bade his accuser add up the reckoning from the pieces. Then, turning to the other senators, he asked why they demanded an account of the three thousand talents that had been expended, but did not demand an account of the ten thousand talents that they were receiving from Antiochus, and did not even consider how they came to be masters, almost in an instant, of Spain, Libya, and Asia too. He said no more, but the authority that went with his plain speaking silenced both his accuser and the rest of the senate. [*Later, however, Lucius was condemned—though reprieved by a tribune—and Publius voluntarily retired from Rome.*]

B. Cato the Censor*

The personality and attitudes of the elder Cato (the Censor) come through well in this quotation. Pliny describes these as Cato's exact words, from a letter written to his son Marcus.

✓   ✓   ✓

XXIX. 14. I shall speak about those Greek fellows in their proper place, son Marcus, and point out the result of my enquiries at Athens, and convince you what benefit comes from dipping into their literature, and not making a close study of it. They are quite a worthless people and an intractable one. . . . When that race gives us its literature it will corrupt all things, and even all the more if it sends hither its physicians. They have conspired together to murder all foreigners with their physic, but this very thing they do for a fee, to gain credit and to destroy us easily. They are also always dubbing us foreigners [*Greek, barbaroi*] and to fling more filth on us than others they give us the foul nickname of *Opici* [*stupid or clownish*]. I have forbidden you to have dealings with physicians.

* Reprinted by permission of the publisher and The Loeb Classical Library from Pliny, *Natural History,* translated by W. H. S. Jones, Cambridge, Mass.: Harvard University Press, 1963.

C. The Younger Scipio (Aemilianus)*

Polybius accompanied Scipio Aemilianus to Africa in the Third Punic War. This account of the feelings of the Roman general as he destroyed Rome's old and bitter enemy is firsthand. Perhaps a liberal education was weakening the fiber of the Romans already. One cannot imagine that either Scipio's father, Aemilius Paullus, or his adoptive grandfather Africanus would have felt anything more than fierce pride and joy at the sight of Carthage in flames.

XXXIX. 5. At the sight of the city utterly perishing amidst the flames Scipio burst into tears, and stood long reflecting on the inevitable change which awaits cities, nations, and dynasties, one and all, as it does every one of us men. This, he thought, had befallen Ilium, once a powerful city, and the once mighty empires of the Assyrians, Medes, Persians, and that of Macedonia lately so splendid. And unintentionally or purposely he quoted— the words perhaps escaping him unconsciously—

"The day shall be when holy Troy shall fall
   And Priam, lord of spears, and Priam's folk [*Iliad, VI. 448*]."

And on my asking him boldly (for I had been his tutor) what he meant by these words, he did not name Rome distinctly, but was evidently fearing for her, from this sight of the mutability of human affairs. . . .

Another still more remarkable saying of his I may record. . . . [*When he had given the order for firing the town*] he immediately turned round and grasped me by the hand and said, "O Polybius, it is a grand thing, but, I know not how, I feel a terror and dread lest some one should one day give the same order about my own native city."

D. Pompey the Great†

These two glimpses of Pompey, one in 70 B.C. when he was serving as an under-age consul who had held no

* From Polybius, *op. cit.*
† From Plutarch, *op. cit.*

*other office of the cursus honorum, and the other just be-
fore the outbreak of war with Caesar, give some indica-
tion of the character of the man. Pompey was not the
first—nor the last—to be misled by public adulation for
a great figure.*

✓   ✓   ✓

XXII. [*Pompey*] himself in person, too, afforded them
[*the populace*] a most grateful spectacle, when he appeared and craved his discharge from the military service.
For it is an ancient custom among the Romans that the
knights, when they had served out their legal time in the
wars, should lead their horses into the market-place before the two officers called censors and having given an
account of the commanders and generals under whom
they served . . . should be discharged. . . . There were
then sitting in state upon the bench two censors, Gellius
and Lentulus, inspecting the knights, who were passing
by in muster before them, when Pompey was seen coming
down into the forum with all the ensigns of a consul, but
leading his horse in his hand. When he came up, he bade
his lictors make way for him, and so he led his horse to
the bench; the people being all this while in a sort of
amaze, and all in silence, and the censors themselves regarding the sight with a mixture of respect and gratifica-
tion. Then the senior censor examined him: "Pompeius
Magnus, I demand of you whether you have served the
full time in the wars that is prescribed by the law?" "Yes,"
replied Pompey, with a loud voice, "I have served all, and
all under myself as general." The people hearing this gave
a great shout, and made such an outcry for delight, that
there was no appeasing it; and the censors rising from
their judgment-seat accompanied him home to gratify the
multitude who followed after, clapping their hands and
shouting.

*   *   *

LVII. About that time Pompey recovered of a dangerous fit of sickness which seized him at Naples, where the
whole city, upon the suggestion of Praxagoras, made
sacrifices of thanksgiving to the gods for his recovery. The
neighboring towns likewise happening to follow their
example, the thing then went its course throughout all

Italy, so that there was not a city, either great or small, that did not feast and rejoice for many days together. And the company of those that came from all parts to meet him was so numerous that no place was able to contain them, but the villages, seaport towns, and the very highways were all full of people, feasting and sacrificing to the gods. Nay, many went to meet him with garlands on their heads, and flambeaux in their hands, casting flowers and nosegays upon him as he went along; so that this progress of his, and reception, was one of the noblest and most glorious sights imaginable. And yet it is thought that this very thing was not one of the least causes and occasions of the civil war. . . . Pompey was so puffed up and led on into such a careless security that he could not choose but laugh at those who seemed to fear a war; and when some were saying that if Caesar should march against the city they could not see what forces there were to resist him, he replied with a smile, bidding them be in no concern, "for," said he, "whenever I stamp with my foot in any part of Italy there will rise up forces enough in an instant, both horse and foot."

— Reading No. 16 —

THE ARBITRARY POLICY OF SULLA

A. The Battle of the Colline Gate, 82 B.C.

1.*

From the time of Gaius Gracchus most Italians looked to the populares *rather than to* optimate *leaders in Rome to do something about their grievances. They wanted citizenship. After they got this, in the Social war, optimate*

* From Velleius Paterculus, *Compendium of Roman History*, translated by J. S. Watson (Harper's Classical Library), 1855.

politicians tried to keep them in a subordinate position in the citizen-assemblies; popularis *politicians usually supported them. It is not surprising that they—the Samnites, especially—joined* popularis *leaders against Sulla (who had fought against them in the final stages of the Social war). This passage (though of uncertain source, perhaps even invented by Velleius) shows plausibly enough their bitterness.*

✓   ✓   ✓

II. 27. At this time, Pontius Telesinus, a Samnite general, a man of great spirit and activity in the field, and a thorough enemy to all the Roman name, having assembled about forty thousand young men of the greatest bravery, and the most determined obstinacy in continuing the war, maintained, in the consulship of Carbo and Marius [*82 B.C., this was an adoptive son of the great Marius*], on the first of November, a hundred and eleven years ago, such a struggle with Sulla at the Colline gate, as brought both him and the republic into utmost peril; nor was the state in more imminent danger when it beheld the camp of Hannibal within three miles of the city, than on that day when Telesinus, hurrying through the ranks of his army, exclaimed that the last day of Rome was come, and exhorted them with a loud voice to pull down and destroy the city, adding, that those wolves, the devourers of Italian liberty, would never cease from ravaging, until the woods in which they took refuge were hewn down. At length, after the first hour of the night, the Roman troops took breath and those of the enemy retired. Next day Telesinus was found mortally wounded, but wearing the look of a conqueror rather than that of a man at the point of death. Sulla ordered his head to be cut off . . . and displayed. . . .

2.*

The policy of Sulla after the battle of the Colline gate was to be brutal; this passage shows how it began. It also indicates why the Senate was so compliant to his wishes.

✓   ✓   ✓

* From Plutarch, *op. cit.*

XXX. Sulla, hearing . . . that most of the enemy was destroyed, came to Antemna by break of day [*Crassus had pursued survivors there*], where three thousand of the besieged having sent forth a herald, he promised to receive them to mercy on condition they did the enemy mischief in coming over. Trusting to his word, they fell foul on the rest of their companions, and made a great slaughter of one another. Nevertheless, Sulla gathered together in the circus, as well these as other survivors of the party, to the number of six thousand, and just as he commenced speaking to the senate, in the temple of Bellona, proceeded to cut them down by men appointed for the service. The cry of so vast a multitude put to the sword in so narrow a space, was naturally heard some distance, and startled the senators. He, however, continuing his speech with a calm and unconcerned countenance, bade them listen to what he had to say and not busy themselves with what was doing out of doors; he had given directions for the chastisement of some offenders. This gave the most stupid of the Romans to understand that they had merely exchanged, not escaped, tyranny.

B. Cicero Defies an Agent of Sulla (About 80 B.C.)*

The elder S. Roscius had been killed and then proscribed afterward through the agency of a freedman of Sulla, Chrysogonus. Fearing apparently that the younger Roscius might be able to reacquire his property, Chrysogonus had the man prosecuted for the murder of his own father. Cicero, as a young orator, could perhaps hope to defend the man with impunity. Older and more experienced advocates refused to undertake the defense. The victory helped to make Cicero's political future bright.

This passage shows that greed caused the proscription of some wealthy persons. It also indicates how men could become rich by buying up land at an ill-publicized auction which was really a farce.

✶   ✶   ✶

VII. When this Sextus Roscius was at Ameria, . . . the son, diligently attending to the farm, . . . at Rome,

---

* From Cicero, *For Sextius Roscius,* translated by C. D. Yonge (Bohn Classical Library), 1900.

Sextus Roscius [*senior*], returning home after supper, is slain near the Palatine baths. I hope from this very fact, that it is not obscure on whom the suspicion of the crime falls; . . . Four days after this happened, news of the deed is brought to Chrysogonus to the camp of Lucius Sulla at Volaterra. The greatness of his fortune is pointed out to him, the excellence of his farms—for he left behind him thirteen farms, which nearly all border on the Tiber—the poverty and desolate condition of his son is mentioned; they point out that, as the father of this man, Sextus Roscius, a man so magnificent and so popular, was slain without any trouble, this man, imprudent and unpolished as he was, and unknown at Rome, might easily be removed. They promise their assistance for this business; not to detain you longer, O judges, a conspiracy is formed.

VIII. As at this time there was no mention of a proscription, and as even those who had been afraid of it before, were returning and thinking themselves now delivered from their dangers, the name of Sextus Roscius, a man most zealous for the nobility, is proscribed and his goods sold; Chrysogonus is the purchaser; three of his finest farms are given to Capito [*a fellow conspirator*] for his own and he possesses them to this day; all the rest of his property that fellow Titus Roscius seized in the name of Chrysogonus, as he says himself. This property worth six millions of sesterces, is bought for two thousand.

I well know, O judges, that all this was done without the knowledge of Lucius Sulla; and it is not strange that while he is surveying at the same time both the things which are past, and those which seem to be impending; when he alone has the authority to establish peace, and the power of carrying on war; when all are looking to him alone, and he alone is directing all things; when he is occupied incessantly by such numerous and such important affairs that he cannot breathe freely, it is not strange, I say, if he fails to notice some things; especially when so many men are watching his busy condition, and catch their opportunity of doing something of this sort the moment he looks away. To this is added, that although he is fortunate, as indeed he is, yet no man can have such good fortune, as in a vast household to have no one, whether slave or freedman, of worthless character. In the meantime Titus Roscius, excellent man, the agent of Chrysogonus, comes to Ameria; he enters on this man's farm; turns this miserable man, overwhelmed with grief, who had not yet performed all the ceremonies of his father's funeral, naked out of his house, and drives him headlong from his paternal hearth and household gods; he himself becomes the owner of abundant wealth. He who had been in great poverty when he had only his own property, became, as is usual, indolent when in possession of the property of another; he carried many things openly off to his own house; he removed still more privily, he gave no little abundantly and extravagantly to his assistants; the rest he sold at a regular auction.

— Reading No. 17 —

CICERO: HIS HOPES
FOR THE REPUBLIC

Cicero as consul thought that the Catilinarian conspiracy had frightened the powerful equestrians and made them see that their best interests were identical with those of the optimates, *who controlled the Senate. He hoped to persuade the* optimates *to keep these equestrians, with their money and influence, safely in the fold. If at the same time the highest offices could be kept open to talent from the equestrian order* [he was himself an example of what he hoped for], *then perhaps a sound coalition of all the good* [boni] *could be formed. This was Cicero's* concordia ordinum. *Such a harmony he thought would have the support of all Italy. But friction arose between the* optimates *and the equestrians. At the same time, intransigent senators like Cato were alienating powerful men like Crassus and Pompey. The result was the dashing*

*of Cicero's hopes and the formation of the first trium-
virate in 60 B.C.*

✓ ✓ ✓

A. Reports from Rome, 61 B.C.*

*These passages report some well-known political activ-
ity. The second passage shows also how Cicero in his not
inconsiderable egotism failed to see that Pompey was
irritated rather than pleased with his praise of himself;
for Pompey's egotism was even greater than Cicero's. It
was Clodius, seeking a love affair with Caesar's wife, who
invaded Caesar's house during religious ceremonies excluding men.*

✓ ✓ ✓

1.

I. 13. No doubt you have heard that, when the sacrifice
[*to the Bona Dea*] was taking place in Caesar's house, a
man in women's clothes got in; and that after the Vestal
Virgins had performed the sacrifice afresh, the matter was
mentioned in the House by Cornificius. Note that he was
the prime mover and none of us. Then a resolution was
passed, the matter was referred to the Virgins and the
priests, and they pronounced it a sacrilege. So the consuls were directed by the House to bring in a bill about it.
Caesar has divorced his wife. Piso's friendship for Clodius
is making him do his best to have the bill shelved, though
he is the person [*as consul*] who has to bring it forward
under the House's orders—and a bill for sacrilege too!
Messalla at present takes a strict view of the case. The
conservatives [*boni viri*] are dropping out of it under
persuasion from Clodius. Gangs of rowdies are being
formed. I, who at first was a perfect Lycurgus, am daily
cooling down. Cato, however, is pressing the case with
energy. . . . Your friend [*Pompey*] . . . is now parad-
ing his affection for me openly and ostentatiously; but in
his heart of hearts he is envious, and he does not disguise
it very well. He is totally lacking in courtesy, candor, in

* Reprinted by permission of the publisher and The Loeb
   Classical Library from Cicero, *Letters to Atticus,* trans-
   lated by E. O. Winstedt, Cambridge, Mass.: Harvard
   University Press, 1928.

brilliancy in his politics, as well as in sense of honor, resolution and generosity. . . .

2.

I. 14. I have already written and told you what Pompey's first public speech was like [*after his return from
the East*]. The poor did not relish it, the socialists [*im-
probis = rabble*] thought it pointless, the rich were not
pleased with it, and the conservatives were dissatisfied:
so it fell flat. Then at the instance of the consul Piso, an
untrustworthy tribune, Fufius, must needs trot out Pompey to deliver an harangue. This happened in the Circus
Flaminius, where there was the usual market-day gathering of riff-raff. Fufius asked him whether he agreed with
the proposal that the praetor should have the selection
of the jurymen and then use them as his panel. That of
course was the plan proposed by the Senate in Clodius'
trial for sacrilege. To this Pompey replied *en grand
seigneur* that he felt and always had felt the greatest respect for the Senate's authority; and very longwinded he
was about it. Afterwards the consul Messalla asked Pompey in the Senate for his opinion on the sacrilege and the
proposed bill. He delivered a speech eulogizing the
Senate's measures *en bloc,* and said to me as he sat down
at my side, that he thought he had given a sufficiently
clear answer to "those questions." Crassus no sooner saw
that he had won public appreciation, because people
fancied that he approved of my consulship, than up he got
and spoke of it in the most complimentary way. He said
that he owed his seat in the House, his privileges as a
citizen, his freedom and his very life, to me. He never
saw his wife's face, or his home, or his native land, without recognizing the debt he owed to me. But enough. He
worked up with great effect all that purple patch which I
so often use here and there to adorn my speeches, to
which you play Aristarchus [*i.e., the critic*]—the passage
about fire and sword—you know the paints I have on my
palette. I was sitting next to Pompey, and noticed that
he was much affected, possibly at seeing Crassus snap up
the chance of winning popularity, which he had thrown
away, and perhaps at realizing the importance of my
achievements, when he saw that praise of them met with
the Senate's entire approval, especially coming from one

who had all the less necessity to praise me, because in every one of my works he has been censured for Pompey's benefit. Today has done a great deal to cement my friendship with Crassus: but still I gladly received any crumbs Pompey let fall openly or covertly. As for me, ye gods, how I showed off before my new listener Pompey! Then, if ever, my flow of rounded periods, my easy transitions, my antitheses, my constructive arguments stood me in good stead. In a word, loud applause! For the gist of it was the importance of the Senatorial order, its unison with the knights [*equestri*], the concord of all Italy, the paralysed remains of the conspiracy, peace and plenty. You know how I can thunder on a subject like that.

3.

I. 16. You want to know next what is the present state of public affairs and how I am getting on. We thought that the condition of the Republic had been set on a firm footing . . . and that its preservation was secured and established by the influence of my consulship. But, let me tell you, unless some god remembers us, it has been dashed from our grasp by this one trial [*of Clodius for sacrilege*], if one can call it a trial, when thirty of the most worthless scoundrels in Rome have blotted out right and justice for filthy lucre. . . .

4.

I. 17. The political position is wretched, rotten, and unstable. I expect you have heard that our friends the knights have almost had a rupture with the Senate. The first point that seriously annoyed them was the publication of a senatorial decree for an investigation into any cases of bribery of jurymen. . . .

Here is another intolerable piece of petulance on the part of the knights; yet I have not only put up with it, but forwarded their cause. The people who farmed the province of Asia from the censors [*i.e., some publicani*], complained in the Senate that their avariciousness had led them to pay too high a price for it, and requested to have the lease annulled. I was their chief supporter, or rather the second, for it was Crassus who encouraged them to venture on the demand. It is a scandalous affair, a disgraceful request. . . . There was considerable danger that if they met with a refusal they might have severed their connection with the Senate entirely. I . . . discoursed freely on the dignity and harmony of the two orders. . . . So I am keeping to our policy and plan, and preserving to the best of my ability that harmony [*concordia*] which I have welded. . . .

B. Cicero's Moderate Spirit (About 55 B.C.)*

This reading shows that Cicero recognized the need for give-and-take in any constitutional government. He was not only willing to put up with the idiosyncrasies of a Cato and the greed of some publicans; he also would put up with assemblies led by factious tribunes. It will be seen that assemblies such as he described were neither made up of a majority of the responsible citizenry nor representative of all Romans.

↗   ↗   ↗

IV. At all comitia, and especially at those held for the election of aediles, it is the party spirit of the people, and not their deliberate judgment, which bears sway; their votes are coaxed out of them, not extorted by merit; the voters are more apt to consider what obligations they themselves are under to each individual, than what benefits the republic had received in his hands. But if you insist on it, that it is their deliberate judgment, then you must not annul it, but bear it. "The people has decided wrongly." Still it has decided. "It ought not to have decided so." Still it had the power. "I will not bear it." But many most illustrious and wise citizens have borne it. For this is the inalienable privilege of a free people, and especially of this the chief people of the world, the lord and conqueror of all nations, to be able by their votes to give or to take away what they please to or from any one. And it is our duty,—ours, I say, who are driven about by the winds and waves of this people, to bear the whims of the people with moderation, to strive to win over their affections when alienated from us, to retain them when we have won them, to tranquillize them when in a state of

* From Cicero, *For C. Plancius,* translated by C. D. Yonge (Bohn Classical Library), 1886.

agitation. If we do not think honors of any great consequence, we are not bound to be subservient to the people; if we do strive for them, then we must be unwearied in soliciting them.

C. The *Concordia:* A Later Version (Late 50's B.C.)*

Cicero now believed that there was a need for a strong hand at the helm—like that of Scipio Aemilianus (here called Africanus) in the Gracchan period. Perhaps he was thinking of Pompey. It has been plausibly suggested that Augustus was influenced by Cicero's ideas. The section preceding this is missing.

II. 42. 69. Then Laelius said: I now see the sort of politician you require, on whom you would impose the office and task of government, which is what I wished to understand.

He must be an almost unique specimen, said Africanus, for the task which I set him comprises all others. He must never cease from cultivating and studying himself, that he may excite others to imitate him, and become, through the splendor of his talents and enterprises, a living mirror to his countrymen. For as in flutes and harps, and in all vocal performances, a certain unison and harmony must be preserved amid the distinctive tones, which cannot be broken or violated without offending experienced ears; and as this concord and delicious harmony is produced by the exact gradation and modulation of dissimilar notes; even so, by means of the just apportionment of the highest, middle, and lower classes, the state is maintained in concord and peace by the harmonic subordination of its discordant elements: and thus, that which is by musicians called harmony in song, answers and corresponds to what we call concord in the state—concord, the strongest and loveliest bond of security in every commonwealth, being always accompanied by justice and equity.

* From Cicero, *On the Republic, loc. cit.*

MOB VIOLENCE IN THE FORUM*

This letter from Marcus Cicero to his brother Quintus describes events in 56 B.C. Pompey had apparently called a contio *or informal assembly to discuss a bill he intended to introduce. Clodius certainly was not interested in maintaining the triumvirate at this point. The violence was all too typical of assemblies in the late Republic.*

✓   ✓   ✓

II. 3. On the 6th of February Milo appeared; Pompey spoke, or rather, intended to speak; for as soon as he was on his legs the mob in Clodius's pay raised a disturbance which lasted throughout his whole speech; and in such a manner that he was hindered from being heard, not merely by the noise, but by reproaches and abuse. When he had summed up what he had been saying (for in that matter he behaved with courage enough; he was not deterred from proceeding; he said all that he meant to say; and, indeed, there were moments when he was heard in silence; and he continued to the end with great authority; but when he had summed up,) up rose Clodius, when such a shout was raised against him by our party, for we determined to pay him off, that he was master neither of his senses, nor of his expressions, nor of his countenance. This scene was continued till two o'clock, Pompey having scarcely finished his peroration at twelve, while every sort of abuse, and even the most obscene verses, were uttered in the way of attack upon Clodius and Clodia [*sister of Clodius, reputedly of loose morals; the "Lesbia" of Catullus*]. He, furious with passion, and pale with terror, amid the uproar, addressed questions to his mob: "Who was it that was killing the people with famine?" The mob

* From Cicero, *Letters to His Brother Quintus, loc. cit.*

replied, "Pompey." "Who was it that wanted to go to Alexandria?" They replied again, "Pompey." "Whom did they wish to go?" They answered, "Crassus." And he, on this occasion, was present with Milo; but with a disposition far from friendly. At about three o'clock, as if a signal had been given, Clodius's mob began to spit upon our party. Indignation rose to a great height; they began to press on in order to drive us from our seats. A rush was made upon them by our party; and a flight of the mob took place. Clodius was driven from the rostrum, and we too then fled, lest we should meet with any accident in the confusion. The senate was summoned to the senate-house; Pompey went home.

— Reading No. 19 —

THE "LIBERATORS"—ASSASSINS OF CAESAR

A. The "Liberators" and the *Populus*, 44 B.C.*

Although this description of the Roman people—or rather, the populace resident in Rome—at the time of Caesar's assassination was written two centuries after the fact, it, nevertheless, shows an acute perception of the makeup of that crowd. A careful reading of this passage will throw light on many events of the history of Rome both before and after the Ides of March, 44 B.C.

ᵧ   ᵧ   ᵧ

II. 17. 120. [*The assassins of Caesar*] hastened up to the Capitol with their gladiators. There they took counsel and decided to bribe the populace, hoping that if some

* From Appian, *Civil Wars,* translated by H. White (Bohn Classical Library), 1899.

would begin to praise the deed others would join in from love of liberty and longing for the Republic. They thought that the Roman people were still exactly the same as they had heard that they were at the time when the elder Brutus expelled the kings. They did not perceive that they were counting on two incompatible things, namely, that people could be lovers of liberty and bribe-takers at the same time. The latter class were much easier to find of the two, because the government had been corrupt for a long time. The plebeians were now much mixed with foreign blood, freedmen had equal rights of citizenship with them, and slaves were dressed in the same fashion as their masters. Except in the case of the senatorial rank the same costume was common to slaves and to free citizens. Moreover the distribution of grain to the poor, which took place in Rome only, drew thither the lazy, the beggars, the vagrants of all Italy. The multitude of discharged soldiers no longer returned one by one to native places as formerly . . . but were sent in groups to unjust allotments of lands and houses belonging to others. These were now encamped in temples and sacred enclosures under one standard, and one person appointed to lead them to their colony, and as they had already sold their own belongings preparatory to their departure they were in readiness to be bought for any purpose.

B. The Motives of Brutus*

Lucius Annaeus Seneca (d. A.D. 65) understood well that the Republic was already dead in Caesar's day and that the "liberators" who assassinated the great dictator were attempting a hopeless task when they tried to restore it.

✦   ✦   ✦

II. 20. It is an oft-debated question whether Marcus Brutus ought to have received his life from the hands of the deified Julius [Caesar] when in his opinion it was his duty to kill him. The reason that led him to kill Caesar I shall discuss elsewhere, for, although in other respects he

* Reprinted by permission of the publisher and The Loeb Classical Library from Seneca, *Moral Epistles,* "On Benefits, "translated by J. W. Basore, Cambridge, Mass.: Harvard University Press, 1935.

was a great man, in this particular he seems to me to have acted very wrongly, and to have failed to conduct himself in accordance with Stoic teaching. Either he was frightened by the name of king, though a state reaches its best condition under the rule of a just king, or he still hoped that liberty could exist where the rewards both of supreme power and of servitude were so great, or that the earlier constitution of the state could be restored after the ancient manners had all been lost, that equality of civil rights might still exist and laws maintain their rightful place where there had been so many thousands of men fighting to decide, not whether, but to which of two masters they would be slaves!

— Reading No. 20 —

DETERIORATING RELATIONS BETWEEN OCTAVIAN AND ANTONY, 35-33 B.C.*

Both Octavian and Antony issued propaganda designed to garner public support. Most of our information is slanted in favor of the former. The so-called "Donations of Alexandria" if correctly reported are most interesting (second paragraph).

✓   ✓   ✓

LIV. When Octavia [*sister of Octavian and wife of Antony*] returned from Athens, Caesar [*Octavian*], who considered she had been injuriously treated, commanded her to live in a separate house; but she refused to leave the house of her husband, and entreated him, unless he had already resolved, upon other motives, to make war

* From Plutarch, *Antony, loc. cit.*

with Antony, that he would on her account let it alone;
it would be intolerable to have it said of the two greatest
commanders in the world that they had involved the
Roman people in a civil war, the one out of passion for,
the other out of resentment about, a woman. And her behavior proved her words to be sincere. She remained in
Antony's house as if he were at home in it, and took the
noblest and most generous care, not only of his children
by her, but of those of Fulvia also. She received all the
friends of Antony that came to Rome to seek office or
upon any business, and did her utmost to prefer their requests to Caesar; yet this her honorable deportment did
but, without her meaning it, damage the reputation of
Antony; the wrong he did to such a woman made him
hated.

Nor was the division he made among his sons at Alexandria less unpopular; it seemed a theatrical piece of
insolence and contempt of his country. For assembling
the people in the exercise ground, and causing two golden
thrones to be placed on a platform of silver, the one for
him and the other for Cleopatra, and at their feet lower
thrones for their children, he proclaimed Cleopatra
Queen of Egypt, Cyprus, Libya, and Coele-Syria, and
with her conjointly Caesarion, the reputed son of the
former Caesar, who left Cleopatra with child. His own
sons by Cleopatra were to have the style of king of kings;
to Alexander he gave Armenia and Media, with Parthia,
so soon as it should be overcome; to Ptolemy, Phoenicia,
Syria, and Cilicia. Alexander was brought out before the
people in Median costume, the tiara and upright peak,
and Ptolemy, in boots and mantle and Macedonian cap
done about with the diadem; for this was the habit of the
successors of Alexander, as the other by one of Armenians.
Cleopatra was then, as at other times when she appeared
in public, dressed in the habit of the goddess Isis, and
gave audience to the people under the name of the New
Isis.

LV. Caesar, relating these things in the senate, and
often complaining to the people, excited men's minds
against Antony, and Antony also sent messages of accusa-
tion against Caesar. The principal of his charges were
these: first, that he had not made any division with him
of Sicily, which was lately taken from Pompey; secondly,

that he had retained the ships he had lent him for the war; thirdly, that, after deposing Lepidus, their colleague, he had taken for himself the army, governments, and revenues formerly appropriated to him; and lastly, that he had parcelled out almost all Italy amongst his own soldiers, and left nothing for his. Caesar's answer was as follows: that he had put Lepidus out of government because of his own misconduct; that what he had got in war he would divide with Antony, so soon as Antony gave him a share of Armenia; that Antony's soldiers had no claims in Italy, being in possession of Media and Parthia, the acquisitions which their brave actions under their general had added to the Roman empire.

BIBLIOGRAPHY

Adcock, F. E., *The Roman Art of War Under the Republic,* Cambridge, Mass., 1940.

————, *Roman Political Ideas and Practice,* Ann Arbor, 1959.

Altheim, F., *A History of Roman Religion,* New York, 1938.

Arnold, E. V., *Roman Stoicism,* London, 1911.

Badian, E., *Foreign Clientelae,* 264-70 B.C., Oxford, 1958.

Bailey, C., *Phases in the Religion of Ancient Rome,* Berkeley, 1932.

Beloch, K. J., *Römische Geschichte bis zum Beginn der Punischen Kriege,* Berlin, 1926.

Bloch, G., and Carcopino, J., *La république romaine de 133 à 44 av. J.-C.;* I. *Des Gracques à Sulla,* Paris, 1929; II. *César,* Paris, 1936.

Bloch, R., *Origins of Rome,* London, 1960.

Boak, A. E. R., and Sinningen, W. G., *A History of Rome to 565 A.D.,* 5th ed., New York, 1965.

Botsford, G. V., *The Roman Assemblies,* New York, 1909.

Buchan, J., *Julius Caesar,* London, 1932.

Carcopino, J., *Autour des Gracques,* Paris, 1928.

Cary, M., *A History of Rome Down to the Age of Constantine,* 2nd ed., London, 1954.

Fowler, W. W., *The Religious Experience of the Roman People from the Earliest Times to the Age of Augustus,* New York, 1911.

————, *Social Life at Rome in the Age of Cicero,* London, 1908.

Frank, T. *Aspects of Social Behavior in Ancient Rome,* Cambridge, Mass., 1932.

————, *Economic History of Rome,* 2nd ed., Baltimore, 1927.

————, *Life and Literature in the Roman Republic,* Berkeley, 1930.

————, *Roman Imperialism,* New York, 1914.

Gelzer, M., *Die Nobilität der römischen Republik,* Berlin, 1912.

Göhler, J., *Rom und Italien,* Breslau, 1939.

Greenidge, A. H. J., *The Legal Procedure of Cicero's Time,* Oxford, 1901.

————, *Roman Public Life,* London, 1901.

Grimal, P., *Le siècle des Scipiòns,* Paris, 1953.

Heichelheim, F. M., and Yeo, C. A., *A History of the Roman People,* Englewood Cliffs, N.J., 1962.

Heitland, W. E., *The Roman Republic,* 3 vols., Cambridge, 1923.

Hill, H., *The Roman Middle Class in the Republican Period*, Oxford, 1952.

Homo, L., *Roman Political Institutions*, New York, 1929.

Hus, Alain, *The Etruscans*, New York, 1961.

Jolowicz, H. F., *Historical Introduction to the Study of Roman Law*, 3rd ed., London, 1952.

Jones, A. H. M., *Cities of the Eastern Roman Provinces*, Oxford, 1937.

――――, *Studies in Roman Government and Law*, Oxford, 1960.

Kienast, D., *Cato der Zensor: seine Persönlichkeit und seine Zeit*, Heidelberg, 1954.

Laistner, M. L. W., *The Greater Roman Historians*, Berkeley, 1947.

MacKendrick, P. L., *The Mute Stones Speak*, New York, 1960.

Magie, D., *Roman Rule in Asia Minor*, 2 vols., Princeton, 1950.

Marsh, F. B., *A History of the Roman World from 146 to 30 B.C.* (2nd ed. rev. by H. H. Scullard), London, 1953.

Mattingly, H., *Roman Coins*, 2nd ed., London, 1960.

Mommsen, T., *Roman History*, 5 vols., New York, 1900.

Moore, R. W., *The Roman Commonwealth*, London, 1942.

Oman, C., *Seven Roman Statesmen of the Later Republic*, London, 1902.

Ormerod, H. A., *Piracy in the Ancient World*, London, 1924.

Pais, E., and Bayet, J., *Des origines à l'achèvement de la conquête*, Paris, 1940.

Pallottino, M., *The Etruscans*, Baltimore, 1955.

Scullard, H. H., *A History of the Roman World from 753 to 146 B.C.*, 2nd ed., London, 1951.

――――, *Roman Politics, 220-150 B.C.*, Oxford, 1951.

Sherwin-White, A. N., *The Roman Citizenship*, Oxford, 1939.

Smith, R. E., *The Failure of the Roman Republic*, Cambridge, 1955.

――――, *Service in the Post-Marian Roman Army*, Manchester, 1958.

Stevenson, G. H., *Roman Provincial Administration*, Oxford, 1939.

Swain, J. W., *The Ancient World*, Vol. II, New York, 1950.

Syme, R., *The Roman Revolution*, Oxford, 1939.

Taylor, L. R., *Party Politics in the Age of Caesar*, Berkeley, 1949.

Thiel, J. H., *Studies in the History of Sea-Power in Roman Republican Times*, Amsterdam, 1946.

Volkmann, Hans, *Cleopatra*, London, 1958.

Warmington, B. H., *Carthage*, New York, 1960.

INDEX

190

VAN NOSTRAND ANVIL BOOKS already published

1 *MAKING OF MODERN FRENCH MIND*—Kohn
2 *THE AMERICAN REVOLUTION*—Morris
3 *THE LATE VICTORIANS*—Ausubel
4 *WORLD IN THE 20th CENTURY*—Rev. Ed. Snyder
5 *50 DOCUMENTS OF THE 20th CENTURY*—Snyder
6 *THE AGE OF REASON*—Snyder
7 *MARX AND THE MARXISTS*—Hook
8 *NATIONALISM*—Kohn
9 *MODERN JAPAN*—Rev. Ed. Tiedemann
10 *50 DOCUMENTS OF THE 19th CENTURY*—Snyder
11 *CONSERVATISM*—Viereck
12 *THE PAPACY*—Corbett
13 *AGE OF THE REFORMATION*—Bainton
14 *DOCUMENTS IN AMERICAN HISTORY*—Morris
15 *CONTEMPORARY AFRICA*—Rev. Ed. Wallbank
16 *THE RUSSIAN REVOLUTIONS OF 1917*—Curtiss
17 *THE GREEK MIND*—Agard
18 *BRITISH CONSTITUTIONAL HISTORY SINCE 1832*—Schuyler
   and Weston
19 *THE NEGRO IN THE U.S.*—Logan
20 *AMERICAN CAPITALISM*—Hacker
21 *LIBERALISM*—Schapiro
22 *THE FRENCH REVOLUTION, 1789-1799*—Gershoy
23 *HISTORY OF MODERN GERMANY*—Snyder
24 *HISTORY OF MODERN RUSSIA*—Kohn
25 *NORTH ATLANTIC CIVILIZATION*—Kraus
26 *NATO*—Salvadori
27 *DOCUMENTS IN U.S. FOREIGN POLICY*—Brockway
28 *AMERICAN FARMERS' MOVEMENTS*—Shannon
29 *HISTORIC DECISIONS OF SUPREME COURT*—Swisher
30 *MEDIEVAL TOWN*—Mundy and Riesenberg
31 *REVOLUTION AND REACTION 1848-1852*—Bruun
32 *SOUTHEAST ASIA AND WORLD TODAY*—Buss
33 *HISTORIC DOCUMENTS OF W. W. I*—Snyder
34 *HISTORIC DOCUMENTS OF W. W. II*—Langsam
35 *ROMAN MIND AT WORK*—MacKendrick
36 *SHORT HISTORY OF CANADA*—Masters
37 *WESTWARD MOVEMENT IN U.S.*—Billington
38 *DOCUMENTS IN MEDIEVAL HISTORY*—Downs
39 *HISTORY OF AMERICAN BUSINESS*—Cochran
40 *DOCUMENTS IN CANADIAN HISTORY*—Talman
41 *FOUNDATIONS OF ISRAEL*—Janowsky
42 *MODERN CHINA*—Rowe
43 *BASIC HISTORY OF OLD SOUTH*—Stephenson
44 *THE BENELUX COUNTRIES*—Eyck
45 *MEXICO AND THE CARIBBEAN*—Hanke
46 *SOUTH AMERICA*—Hanke
47 *SOVIET FOREIGN POLICY, 1917-1941*—Kennan
48 *THE ERA OF REFORM, 1830-1860*—Commager
49 *EARLY CHRISTIANITY*—Bainton
50 *RISE AND FALL OF THE ROMANOVS*—Mazour
51 *CARDINAL DOCUMENTS IN BRITISH HISTORY*—Schuyler and
   Weston
52 *HABSBURG EMPIRE 1804-1918*—Kohn
53 *CAVOUR AND UNIFICATION OF ITALY*—Salvadori
54 *ERA OF CHARLEMAGNE*—Easton and Wieruszowski
55 *MAJOR DOCUMENTS IN AMERICAN ECONOMIC HISTORY,
   Vol. I*—Hacker
56 *MAJOR DOCUMENTS IN AMERICAN ECONOMIC HISTORY,
   Vol. II*—Hacker
57 *HISTORY OF THE CONFEDERACY*—Vandiver
58 *COLD WAR DIPLOMACY*—Graebner
59 *MOVEMENTS OF SOCIAL DISSENT IN MODERN EUROPE*—
   Schapiro
60 *MEDIEVAL COMMERCE*—Adelson
61 *THE PEOPLE'S REPUBLIC OF CHINA*—Buss
62 *WORLD COMMUNISM*—Hook
63 *ISLAM AND THE WEST*—Hitti